GILGAMESH CON/QUEST

The epic dramatized in seven scenes

Title: Gilgamesh Con/Quest: The epic dramatized in seven scenes
Copyright © 2025 by Kairios Press

Gilgamesh Con/Quest, The epic dramatized in seven scenes by Ralph Blasting and Mahmood Karimi Hakak
Foreword by Ralph Blasting
Preface by Mahmood Karimi Hakak
"TSU Stages Ancient Epic" by R. M. Grau
"Introduction to the Gilgamesh Epic" by Michael B. Dick
"The Goddess Would Like a Word" by Cheryl De Ciantis
Original Music by Wendy Balder
Book Design and Cover Illustration by Cheryl De Ciantis

ISBN: 978-0-9857379-6-2

Published 2025 in the United States by
Kairios Press
8853 E Buckboard Rd
Tucson, AZ 85749 USA

GILGAMESH CON/QUEST

The epic dramatized in seven scenes

Written for the stage by

Mahmood Karimi Hakak

and

Ralph Blasting

Based on the translation by
John Gardner and John Maier

Kairios Press

TUCSON, ARIZONA

In loving memory of Shaparak

Contents

Acknowledgments

Gilgamesh Con/quest, like many other original works of theatre, is the result of collaborative efforts of a group of artists. However, unlike many other plays it did not begin with a prepared script. Rather, it was initiated out of a desperate attempt of a teacher trying to keep his job. You will read more about that in the Preface, so here let me acknowledge those who helped make this project come to fruition. First, I have to thank my friend and colleague Ralph Blasting for taking the leap with me. Then let me recognize the intelligence of the late Maravene Loeschke, our department chair, who trusted two young faculty members' untested creative process and allowed Ralph and me team-teach a yearlong course whose validity and success with undergraduate students was uncertain. However, I am most thankful to the students who supported our inspiration by registering for a class that was as new to them as it was to us. They gave their all to improvisations, experimentation, and the hard work of making a new play. I also thank Wendy Balder for her original music, without which the play would not have been as engaging.

Now, some thirty years later, we are putting the words produced through this totally collaborative process on paper. Our starting point was the English version of the epic of Gilgamesh, by John Gardner and John Maier (1984). I thank my colleague Michael Dick for his informative introduction to the Gilgamesh Epic. I am deeply grateful to my friend Cheryl De Ciantis, not only for her enlightening essay on Ishtar, but also for her tireless efforts in editing and designing this book. I also appreciate my friend Roja Ebrahimi's help in the first layout of this book. Lastly, both Ralph and I are deeply grateful to our wives, Eli and Laurie, whose love, support, and encouragement provided fuel and energy all through this project.

Mahmood Karimi Hakak

Foreword

As I write this, a close family member is beginning the process of dying. My best friend Mahmood calls. He talks about a play we created together over 30 years ago, based on the epic of Gilgamesh. The story is five thousand years old and is a tale of friendship, mortality, and enduring love. Should we publish the script after all these years, and would I write an introduction about how it came to be?

Gilgamesh was young and brash and bold, as were the undergraduate actors who first performed the play. He dared to enter the cedar forest guarded by the monster Humbaba, just as they dared to enter the rehearsal process for new play based on the world's oldest epic and created through improvised movement. Both projects seemed egocentric and foolhardy. It would be much better to stay at home, tend to your flocks and crops, and die peacefully; much better to choose a script off the shelf. But Gilgamesh was driven to be extraordinary, the first hero to exhibit the hubris that we have come to both fear and admire.

He was not alone—at least, not in the early days. Enkidu, his best friend and only equal, went with him to face gods and monsters together. They fought the giant of the cedar forest and won. This angered the gods, who sent the Bull of Heaven to destroy them—but they stood together and won again. The gods, unable to conquer this pair by force, turned to slow suffering. And they knew that the suffering of your loved one is more painful than your own. "Enkidu shall die. His one friend and companion shall be to Gilgamesh the image and mirror of death." And so Gilgamesh—and our student actors, and we ourselves—learn about power and its limits, the strategies of the authorities, suffering and empathy, loyalty and love.

My loved one is in his hospital bed. His rest is interrupted by a sudden groan. He cries out, briefly. I ask "What is wrong? What hurts?" "Nothing, nothing." He rests again, then writhes, trying to comfort a body that will not be comforted; he groans and twists, then rests again, his breathing unsteady.

A fifth day and a sixth Enkidu lay on his bed, and did not move.
A seventh day, an eighth the sickness held him.
Inside his body a fire raged, though his skin was cold to the touch.
Gilgamesh asked "How can I protect him from an evil unseen?"
The wounds were invisible, but the pain so strong
That breath came hard, and the light of his eyes grew dim.

After Enkidu was gone, Gilgamesh sought for meaning to the ends of the earth. He crossed into the Underworld. He briefly grasped the secret of life, only to have it slip away. And when he returned to his home, to the city he had built, no one recognized him.

The students worked on the play for a full academic year. Fall semester was spent improvising movements and characters, developing scenes and images in the tradition of Grotowski and Eugenio Barba. Spring rehearsals created the sequences, added music and song, trying to find a final version before opening night. I don't know if it was a good play. I don't know if the audiences were engaged, or moved, or even remember it. Some were confused: "Where is the dramatic arc? The actors are not playing their objectives. What world are we in?" But I read the script again for the first time in 30 years. It was written before 9/11, before the Forever Wars, the mass migrations, before the pandemic, Black Lives Matter, or the efforts to make America great (again). Reading the script reminded me that my best friend is still my best friend, but that we will not share this world forever. It told me that as we grow old, no one will recognize us when we go home. And it reassured me that love—committed, profound, and enduring love—is all that gives this life meaning. I believe that these truths live in the hearts of those who worked on the play. A trace of those truths and those hearts remain in this script. Perhaps it will speak softly to you.

Ralph Blasting, November 2024

Preface

It is no secret that many great theatre productions result from improvisations. However, selecting a play to produce often requires knowledge, research, interest, and perhaps even some thought! Yet in my life in theatre, improvisation has almost always played a role in both creating a theatrical production as well as choosing which play to direct.

Ralph Blasting and I both received our first full-time teaching positions at Towson University in the fall of 1989. Ralph was a fresh Ph.D. from the University of Toronto, and I had been working as a freelance director and designer, while making a living as a cab driver in New York City between my two terminal degrees. We shared a small, windowless office with two metal desks, a filing cabinet, and some shelves. Our relatively comfortable wheeled desk chairs sat back-to-back, making it virtually impossible for both of us to lean back at the same time. A very small table sat next to his desk, with a four-cup coffee maker on it. There was a couch placed next to the entrance door, where our students sat during the office hours. Depending on which one of us the student wanted to meet with, the other person would take a walk.

The couch had another function as well. Every so often, I would take the four-hour drive to NYC to see a play, visit with old friends, and/or have a few well-made drinks. Driving back to Towson, I often arrived around sunrise, and having no one to go home to, I would crash on this couch until Ralph, arriving at 8:30 AM, woke me up to go teach. Sometimes he would kick the couch out of frustration, anger or envy. Our morning greetings began like this:

"Wake up! Wake up" he'd yell, "you're gonna be late for class!"

"What am I teaching?" I'd ask half asleep.

"Directing 1," he'd answer, "get up!!"

With only one eye open, I'd gaze at him both grateful and annoyed, and ask, "What are we doing in class today?"

He'd take a quick look at the notes spread over my desk. "The students are presenting their concept papers for the scenes they are to direct," he'd remind me with a gentle yet pitiful voice. The rest was routine; a walk to the bathroom, a splash of water on my face, running my wet hands through my hair, and there I was in the studio, holding a strong dark coffee that my office-mate had just made, ready to tackle the task of the day.

Every Tuesday afternoon we had a faculty meeting when our Chair, the late Maravene Loeschke, updated us on the University's news, department affairs, and students' progress. It was in one of these meetings during the Spring 1990, when Mar, as we used to call her, praising my recent production of A Midsummer Night's Dream, asked, "Well, Mahmood, what are you going to direct next?"

I had forgotten that in this meeting we were to address the next season's theatre productions, their directors, dramaturges, designers, etc., and, not unlike many other meetings, I was totally unprepared. So, her question took me by surprise. In the few seconds it took to respond, my mind raced through every play I had ever read, productions I had seen, and even those I hadn't read or seen, but heard about. Nothing stuck to my mind. She was about to repeat her question, when I heard myself say "Gilgamesh!" I was as surprised hearing this title as everyone else in the room, although the puzzling looks on my colleagues' faces was a clear indication that no one else was familiar with the epic.

I continued almost unconsciously,

"I have been thinking about doing a production of Gilgamesh."

"What is Gilgamesh?" asked our illustrious Chair.

"Well, Gilgamesh is an epic poem," I responded, "it is the oldest poem in human history."

"Oh, and who is the play by?" said Madam Chair.

I responded hurriedly, "There is no play that I know of."

There was a strange look on her face, and the face of other faculty. Ralph glanced at me with an upset look as if to say, "You are not making any sense!" So, before the next question came my way, I added "We are writing a play based on this epic poem." There was an uneasy silence for a few seconds, then with a mixture of curiosity and doubt, Mar asked, "And, who is WE?" Ralph was sitting on my left, still staring at me with a vague smile as if enjoying my falling into my own trap. "It is going to be a collaboration," I said, "Ralph is writing the script!"

I will never forget the look on his face. His jaw dropped, his eyes bulged, and his face turned into the face of someone who is ready to commit a murder right there and then. But luckily, before he had a chance to expose my lie, Maravene, came to my rescue.

"Oh, Ralph! I didn't know you are a playwright too." Fearing that Ralph is going to be his honest self again, I jumped in with a response, "Oh, no, he is not." Adding "This is going to be his first script!" The Chair, who often openly praised Ralph's intelligence and scholarship, concluded, "Well, this is wonderful! An original production of Gilgamesh!" Then turning to others, she half-jokingly added, "I think we all should read the actual poem to make sure Ralph is staying true to the text." Then went on to continue with the other agenda items.

We hadn't completely entered our office when Ralph, slamming the door behind us, almost attacked me. "What are you doing saying I am writing the play," he screamed, "I don't even know what the damn thing is," throwing his hands up in the air, he continued with ridicule, "You are absolutely crazy!" Well, I was in those days, and somehow I want to think I still am. I did try to reassure my friend and colleague that he would enjoy the project, but he would not have it. Taking his brown leather shoulder bag, he stormed out of the office, slamming the door behind him.

In the weeks to come we did not talk about whether he was going to work on the script. Rather, we brainstormed about how we could make this project happen. Finally we decided to team-teach an experimental theatre course the next Fall where I would conduct improvisations on the themes expressed in the Gilgamesh poem, and he would write scenes based on the events described. It was a three-hour class twice a week, and I think we both enjoyed working with a dozen students exploring ideas, images and actions. The students were generally open to new experimentations and explorations and seemed to like the class. Maravene also stopped by our class from time to time observing her two newest faculty at work.

Ralph and I were constantly exchanging ideas, discussing the events and deciding on the overall plot of the play. Every time Ralph sketched a new scene, we worked on it in class, finding places that worked well, and places that needed improvement. By the end of the Fall semester, we had the skeleton of a play, as well as hundreds of pages of notes. Ralph and I continued working together on the final version of a script over dinners, wine and coffee.

The students who participated in the experimental workshop were automatically cast in the show, and a few more were added to the group through spring auditions. Rehearsals always began with warm-ups and exercises because we knew that the performance would be physically challenging. We continued with guided image improvisations, attempting to bring the students' individual selves to the characters sketched in the epic poem. I drew on my knowledge and experiences of the work of Jerzy Grotowski, Eugenio Barba, and Richard Schechner. In fact, Schechner came to Towson at my invitation to conduct a day of workshops with us. Slowly, the play came into focus, although not without some anxiety from our production crews and colleagues. "Will it be ready?" seemed to be the most common question – a question in some ways antithetical to my whole process. Ready for what? Ready to give an audience a polished and predictable performance with a beginning, middle, and end? Probably not. Ready to invite an audience to share Gilgamesh's struggle to make sense of an unpredictable and dangerous world, to seek and find friendship, to come to terms with his own mortality, each night, in the moment? Absolutely.

Was it a success? In college theatre, success is measured not only by ticket sales but also by the value of the experience for the students. The show sold well enough. Some reactions from colleagues and critics were positive, some negative. But I have no doubt, even after all this time, that the cast experienced a unique process of improvisational theatre which challenged and expanded their awareness of their own capabilities. It was an experience worth remembering, based on a poem that has endured for millennia. I am pleased to offer this script to you as a shadow of that performance. I hope that the shadows will dance.

Mahmood Karimi Hakak

TSU Stages Ancient Epic

"Gilgamesh and Enkidu slaying Humbaba at the Cedar Forest." 19th-17th century BCE. Vorderasiatisches Museum, Berlin, Germany. Photo by Osama Shukir Muhammed Amin FRCP (Glasg) is licensed under CC BY-SA 4.0.

A man is dying, his body wracked by fever and chills. Another man, healthy and strong, tries in vain to soothe his torment. He holds him in his arms, bathes his neck and forehead with cool water, listens to his ravings. He stares into his friend's eyes trying to understand what is happening, trying to understand what death is, and why the man he loves must be taken from him.

This is the pivotal scene from a new play being produced by the Towson State University Theatre Department as part of the university's Experimental Theatre Festival, and while not about AIDS, it is uncanny how it relates to the emotional and spiritual crisis the disease has brought to the gay community.

Uncanny, because the play is based on the Mesopotamian epic of Gilgamesh, a narrative written approximately 5,000 years ago.

Discovered in the last century on a set of Assyrian tablets, the story speaks with cold, open-eyed wisdom from the age of Sumer. Simple and yet richly enigmatic, it tells of how the semi-divine Gilgamesh, king of Uruk, was challenged, loved, and tempered by Enkidu, the wild man who lived with the animals, how together they vanquished the giant of the forest, mocked Ishtar, and killed the great bull of heaven sent to avenge the chagrined goddess; and finally, how the gods destroyed Enkidu and how Gilgamesh, grief-stricken, journeyed to the ends of the earth seeking to comprehend his own mortality.

Director Mahmood Karimi-Hakak first read the story as a teenager in Iran, and it possessed him. So when, as a new dram professor at TSU, he was asked last year at a department faculty meeting to suggest a project for the students, he proposed staging Gilgamesh.

The idea intrigued Ralph Blasting, who teaches theater history in the department. As a graduate student, he had helped put on medieval mystery cycles and was fascinated by the problem: How do you put something of epic proportions on the stage? Unlike his graduate work, Gilgamesh would involve adapting ancient epic to modern experimental theater. Blasting recalls that a couple of weeks after the faculty meeting, "Mahmood said, 'Well why don't you write it and I'll direct it?'"

Work on the project began last fall in the experimental theater workshop taught by Karimi-Hakak and Blasting. The goal, the director says, was "to come up with a script [for Gilgamesh] through working with actors, improvisations and ideas in collaboration with the students." Blasting finished a working version of the script in mid-January, and rehearsals began, though adjustments and editing have continued right up to the end of February.

How do you introduce the gods and goddesses, giants and monsters that filled Sumerian hearts with fear onto an American university stage without seeming banal or condescending? Rejecting technical tricks (flashing lights, smoke, etc.), Karimi-Hakak's solution was to work with students to discover "some abstract image" of a given mythological being, "what kind of space he might have occupied," then strive as an ensemble to convey that image.

The most difficult part was "to get the American student to understand the feeling of an epic, the sense of something ancient," the director recalls. He encouraged his actors to discover in themselves "the conjunction between modern man and ancient man," This, he believes, "is something that has to do with our sense of balance and our sense of impulse—something that has to do with our sense of balance and our sense of impulse—something that has little to do with our mind."

The company of 13 actors used many balance exercises, he explains, "hoping that by bringing a balance to one's body we'll be able to somehow convey this idea of balance in the universe" between the three worlds of nature, humanity, and the gods, which Karimi-Hakak sees as the organizing principle of the work.

To judge from the rehearsal I saw last month, the exercises have largely paid off. The production is alive with physicality, the company forming a protean flux of bodies that serves now as a forest, now as a god, now as Enkidu's unearthly torments. Movement and gestures seem drawn from a repertoire blending circus acrobatics, ballet, and yoga.

But perhaps even more problematic for the TSU students than bringing a god to the stage has been understanding the love between Gilgamesh and Enkidu. "This has been one of the most difficult themes we've had to deal with," says Blasting.

Not wanting "to send the audience off on a different track" looking for contemporary American labels to pin on the friends (are they gay lovers or male-bonding jocks?), the company decided early to try to avoid the issue of homosexuality. The heroes' love wasn't, after all, an issue in the original.

"What is important to the play is that Gilgamesh and Enkidu are extremely close," Blasting says. "They complete one another." But he agrees that a striking contemporary parallel to the anguish of Gilgamesh is found in the tragedy of a lover dying of AIDS: "That's the degree of emotional separation that we want to convey."

At the run-through two weeks before the opening, there were naturally many bugs still to be worked out, not the least of which was the need for a clearer definition of the Gilgamesh-Enkidu relationship. But on the whole, the production promises to be imaginative, exciting, and intelligent theater. Karimi-Hakak, Blasting, and the young actors are to be commended for tackling an unusual and ambitious project. One wishes them much success.

–Review by R. M. Grau, March 1991

Introduction to the Gilgamesh Epic

By Michael B. Dick

Fig. 1 - Gilgamesh (right) and Enkidu (left) attack Humbaba. Detail of cylinder seal, c. 7th cent. BCE. Schøyen Collection MS 1989.

Epic of Gilgamesh (SBV) Tablet 1:1–2[1]	
[He who saw the Deep, the] foundation of the country	[ša$_2$ naq-ba i-mu-ru i]š-di ma-a-ti
[who knew. . .] was wise in everything	[X X X-ti i-du]-u$_2$ ka-la-mu ḫa-as-s[u]
Homer's Odyssey, Book 1:1–4[2]	
Sing to me of the man, Muse, the man of twists and turns	ἄνδρα μοι ἔννεπε, μοῦσα, πολύτροπον, ὃς μάλα πολλὰ
driven time and again off course, once he had plundered	πλάγχθη, ἐπεὶ Τροίης ἱερὸν πτολίεθρον ἔπερσεν:
the hallowed heights of Troy.	πολλῶν δ' ἀνθρώπων ἴδεν ἄστεα καὶ νόον ἔγνω,
Many cities of men he saw and learned their minds, many pains he suffered, heartsick on the open sea....	πολλὰ δ' ὅ γ' ἐν πόντῳ πάθεν ἄλγεα ὃν κατὰ θυμόν...

The opening lines in "the Epic of Gilgamesh" recall Homer's beginning of his "Odyssey." William Moran, the late professor of Assyriology at Harvard University, expressed his admiration for the Gilgamesh Epic when he averred:

> Today it [Gilgamesh] takes its place next to the "Iliad" and the "Odyssey," and it is known to students of literature everywhere.[3]

And now it lives on in Ralph Blasting and Mahmood Karimi Hakak's play "Gilgamesh Con/Quest." If poets are the best suitable to esteem other poets, then this correspondence of the Austrian poet Rainer Maria Rilke (1875–1926) with Katharina Kippenberg, the wife of his publisher, fittingly expresses his esteem for the newly discovered and translated Mesopotamian Gilgamesh Epic.

Gilgamesh ist ungeheuer! Ich kenns aus der Ausgabe des Urtextes und rechne es zum Grössesten, das einem widerfahren kann. Von Zeit zu Zeit erzähl ichs dem und jenem, den ganzen Verlauf, und habe jedesmal die erstaunendsten Zuhörer.

Gilgamesh is astounding! I know this from the version of the original text and consider it the best that we can experience.[5] From time to time I tell the whole story to this or that person, and each time I have the most astonished listeners.

"The Epic of Gilgamesh" remains the longest and best-known Akkadian literary work from the ancient Near East.[6] Its fame can be attested both diachronically and synchronically, both vertically through time and horizontally at most contemporary times in its history, which stretches from 2500 BCE to the dramatization found here. It is the longest Epic before Homer's Iliad and Odyssey. "Gilgamesh" is noteworthy in that you can trace its written evolution over two thousand years:

GILGAMESH	APPROXIMATE DATES
Historical Bilgames/Gilgamesh King of Uruk	c. 2750 BCE
Gilgamesh becomes a god & is worshiped	c. 2500 BCE
Individual Sumerian stories about the god Gilgamesh	22nd to 17th centuries BCE
OB Akkadian Epic "šūtur eli šarrī (Surpassing all other Kings)" written in Akkadian (partially preserved)	End of 2nd millennium
Standard Babylonian Version (SBV) in Akkadian attributed to author/scribe Sin-leqe-unnini	1500 BCE

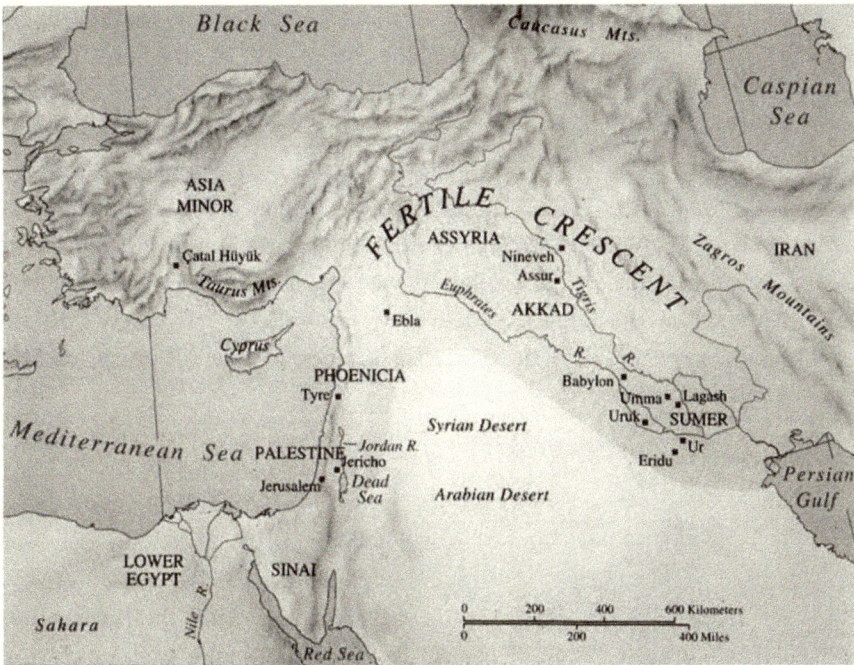

Fig. 2 - Map of Mesopotamia. Source: ar.inspiredpencil.com/pictures-2023

Historicity of a King of Uruk

From the approximate period of B., i.e., the Early Dynastic Period (c. 2750 BCE) we have no contemporary evidence such as a royal inscription from Uruk or from anywhere for B.'s historicity. With one exception, the oldest evidence for B.'s historic kingship of Uruk is weak: The earliest references to Bilgames stem from the Ur III Period, during which time (22nd to 21st century BCE) Sumerian dynasty ruled in the city of Ur. From this period was: 1) the Sumerian King List (SKL);[7] 2) the Tummal Inscription; and 3) the divinization of Gilgamesh with various hymns and prayers.[8]

1) THE SUMERIAN KING LIST

The Sumerian King List (SKL) dates from the end of the third and beginning of the second millennium (i.e., c. six hundred years after B.). Originally composed in Sumerian, it counted him as the fifth king of Uruk who ruled for 126 years:

dbil-ga-mes ab-ba-ni lil-la$_2$ en kul-ab-ba-ke$_4$ mu 2,6 i-ak[9]

Bilgames—his father was a lil-la? (phantom?)— lord of Kullab,[10] he ruled for 126 years.

25

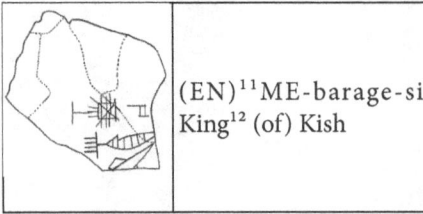

(EN)[11]ME-barage-si King[12] (of) Kish

Of course, many scholars doubt the historicity of the pre-Sargonic rulers.[13] However, the recent discovery of a fragment of an alabaster jar should complicate such doubts. This circumstantial evidence is a short royal inscription from EN.ME.bara$_2$-si, the penultimate Lord (en) of the first dynasty of Kish; according to the SKL this king was the father of King Aka of Kish,[14] with whom B. fought in the Sumerian Poem "Bilgames and Aka" (see below) that established the hegemony of Uruk over Kish. Abandoning the historical, the SKL says he ruled for 900 years!

2) The Tummal Inscription[15]

Fig. 3 - Remnants of the Tummal.
Source: ancientpages.com.

The Tummal Inscription is a repetitive list of kings who contributed to the Tummal shrine for Ninlil in Nippur. Ninlil was the spouse of the main god Enlil, the Tummal was part of his temple complex. Old Babylonian scribal schools frequently used this cuneiform text for students to practice. The text probably dates to the end of the third millennium; its colophon[16] mentions king Ishbi-Erra the founder of the Dynasty of Isin (c. 1953—1717 BCE), the last dynasty on the Sumerian King List. Since Ishbi-Erra founded the dynasty after rebelling against the earlier Ur III dynasty, there were questions of its legitimacy. Nippur, the site of Enlil, king of the Cosmos, was important for the en "lord" to be an overall king (lugal). The Tummal Inscription sought to link this crucial shrine of Enlil to Bilgames, implying the relation of Bilgames to Isin.

King Enmebaraggesi built uru-na-nam, 'The Very City', the house of Enlil; Akka, son of Enme-baraggesi, made Tummal resplendent, he brought Ninlil to Tummal. Tummal was abandoned for the first time.

King Mesannepadda built bur-šu$_2$-šu$_2$.aki 'Covered Jars', the house of Enlil; Meskiagnunna, son of Mesannepadda, made Tummal resplendent, he brought Ninlil to Tummal. Tummal was abandoned for the second time.

26

Bilgames built du$_6$ (u^2)numun$_2$.bur-ra, 'Mound of Rushes', the throne-dais of Enlil; Ur-lugal, son of Bilgames, made Tummal resplendent, he brought Ninlil to Tummal. Tummal was abandoned for the third time.

Nanne built giškiri$_6$.maḫ. (a), 'Sublime Garden', the house of Enlil; Meskiag-Nanna, son of Nanne, made Tummal resplendent, he brought Ninlil to Tummal. Tummal was abandoned for the fourth time.[17]

This list disagrees with the order of the SKL which lists Bilgames as coming right after Ak(k)a son of (en) Mebaraggesi. Although the Tummal Inscription places king Mesannepadda of Ur before Bilgames, it does associate B. with these early kings for which we do have royal inscriptions.

Fig. 4 - Seal of King Messanepadda of Ur (c. 26th century BCE). The man dominating the lions is thought to be Bilgames as master of the animals. University of Pennsylvania. Museum of Archaeology and Anthropology, UPM 31.16.677. Image Source: Wikimedia Commons, attr. Dr. L. Legrain.

3) BILGAMES AS A GOD TO WHOM OMENS AND PRAYERS ARE DIRECTED

Divine Bilgames

Bilgames was regarded as divine as early as Early Dynastic god-lists from ancient Šuruppak (see Fig. 2 map). In the ancient Near East, the gods often presumably communicated with humans by omens, signs with prognostic meaning. These were collected in huge collections divided by the type of omen, e.g., dreams, celestial signs, miscarriages, or the directions of incense smoke, etc. Many of these involved Gilgamesh. Ironically for a chaser after immortality, Gilgamesh became the judge of the Underworld, to whom many prayers and hymns were dedicated.

Fig. 5 - Stone mace-head dedicated to Bilgames as a god. Dated to Ur III around 2112 BCE. His name is preceded by the cuneiform sign for a god (indicated by arrow). Musée du Louvre, département des Antiquités orientales, AO 3761. Commons Image Attribution: Cc-by-sa-3.0-fr.

Lord of the Underworld

dbil$_4$-ga-mes umun ki-t[a..][18]   Bilgames Lord of the Underworld

In the poem "Death of Bilgames" (see below), he is promised the role as judge of the dead as compensation for his having to die.[19] Because of his sea voyage to see Uta-napishti, G. was also regarded as the Mesopotamian psychopomp, ferryman of souls to the Netherworld.

Judge of the Netherworld

dbil-ga-mes gidim-bi-ta ki-ta ug-ga	Bilgames in the form of his ghost, dead in the underworld
GIR$_3$.NITA$_2$ kur-ra ḫe$_2$-ak-e igi-du gidim-(bi) ḫe$_2$-nam	Shall act as governor of the Netherworld, shall be indeed chief of the shades!
di-da mu-un-ku$_5$-da ka-aš-bar ba? -bar-re	He will pass judgment, he shall hand down verdicts,
dug$_4$-ga-a-zu inim dnin-giš-zi-da (d)dumu-zi-da-gin$_7$ ba-e-dugud	What he says (text: "you" say) will carry the same weight as the word of Ningishzida and Dumuzi.[20]

Psychopomp

A psychopomp is a fancy word for the mythological character that ferries dead souls across a river to the Netherworld, e.g., Greek Charon ferrying souls across the River Styx to Hades.

[z]i dGIŠ-gim-maš lu₂ gišma-laḫ	Be oath-bound by the life of Gilgamesh,
[kur-ra-ke₄ ḫe₂-pad₃ [21]	the boatman of the Netherworld.

Omens

In the first of the two following omens, the "renovation" undoubtedly refers to refurbishing the god's statue.

DIŠ dGIŠ-gim-maš u₂-di-iš ki-ṣir libbi ili-šu₂ ip[paṭṭar-šu₂]	If one renovates a divine Gilgamesh, the wrath of one's god will [be dispelled.]
[MAŠ l]i-bu e-pi-ik a-mu-ut dge-el-ga [ša-ma-ḫ]i-ra-am la i-šu-u₃	[If the] heart is massive, it is an omen of Gilgamesh, [who] had no equal.

4) ARCHAEOLOGICAL EVIDENCE

Fig. 6 - Model of Plano-Convex Brick Metropolitan Museum 59.41.2 .API/Public Domain.

There is ambiguous archaeological evidence in some places that shows that below a later wall of Uruk, a much older wall of plano-convex clay bricks (see left) is built that are typical of Early Dynastic building materials (c. 2900–2350 BCE).[22] These might have been the famed walls of Uruk which Bilgames reputedly laid.

This stratigraphy of the thick walls of Uruk shows at the lowest level the presence of lower rows of plano-convex bricks which date from the Early Dynastic Period, which would include the time of Bilgames.

Fig. 7 - Lower level of plano-convex bricks from earliest wall of Uruk. Source: https://wikimapia.org/2066781/Uruk.

SBV of Gilgamesh Epic Tablet 1:18–19:

"Mount up upon the wall of Uruk and roam around! Examine the foundation terrace, check out the brickwork thoroughly...."

Here, are some of the earliest independent Sumerian Bilgames poems preserved.[23] The dates given are of the cuneiform clay documents, undoubtedly the oral stories were much older. The earliest clay tablets date from the Ur III (22nd to 21st century BCE to the 17th-century, many of which were school texts, copying exercises for scribal students. Most ended with a doxology.

SUMERIAN POEM[24]	CONTENT & DOXOLOGY
1) Bilgames and Akka	Bilgames saves Uruk from a takeover by Aka of ki Kish. The doxology is "dBil-ga-meš en kul-aba$_4$ ki-a-ke$_4$ za$_2$-mi-zu dug$_2$-ga-am$_3$ (Bilgames, Lord of Kullab, sweet is your praise.)" The superscript "d" sign before his name indicates he was considered here a god (dingir).
	RELATION TO 7TH CENT. BCE AKKADIAN SBV OF GILGAMESH
	Although Bilgames here is consistent with his heroism elsewhere in the SBV, this poem is not contained in the SBV.
2) Bilgames and the Halub Tree[25]	The incipit of this poem is "u$_4$-ri-a u$_4$-sud$_3$-ra$_2$-ri-a (In those days, in those far distant days)." In the far off days after the gods had apportioned the universe to various gods, Ea was on his way by boat to the Apsu when he was assailed by a storm which caused a Halub tree (an oak?) on the banks of the Euphrates to be uprooted. During a walk one day Inanna came upon the willow and brought it back to her temple in Uruk and replanted it so she could one day make furniture of its wood. As it grew, however, it was beset with evil demons. She asked Bilgames' help to rid the tree; he chopped it down and gave the timber to Inanna for furniture. With the remainder of the wood, he fashioned a ball and mallet.[26] Bilgames rode the men piggy-back—human polo! They played the game incessantly, while the women kept them fed. The women grew tired of the effort and petitioned the gods. A chasm yawned open and swallowed the mallet and the ball. Bilgames could not reach the two objects. Enkidu volunteered to go down to the netherworld to get and return the mallet and ball. Bilgames warns Enkidu about the special etiquette for behavior in the underworld especially regarding Ereshkigal, Queen of the Netherworld. Sadly, the cocky Enkidu Blithely disregards Bilgames' admonitions, and is condemned to remain as a shade in the Underworld. Bilgames petitions the god Enlil to no avail, Enki brings Bilgames' petition to the sun-god Utu who grants Enkidu a

	one-time visitation with Bilgames. As the sun sets, Enkidu visits with Bilgames, who asks Enkidu about the underworld. First, Enkidu tells Bilgames that those who have large families with many sons are happier in the underworld because they have people to send their dead family food and drink. The childless who die are in dire straits. Also people who do not die with their bodies intact will suffer their corporeal impairment in the afterlife. Those who are consumed by fire simply disappear upon their death: no afterlife for them.
	RELATION TO 7TH CENT. BCE AKKADIAN SBV OF GILGAMESH
	Part of this poem (lines 172–), or perhaps a variant of it, appears in Akkadian translation in Tablet XII of the SVB of Gilgamesh.[27] We know this was an intentional addition because tablet XI ends with a catchline for the incipit of tablet XII. In the Sumerian poems Enkidu is more Bilgames' servant than Gilgamesh's bosom brother as in the SBV.
3) Bilgames and Ḫuwawa/ Ḫumbaba[28]	In fear of death, Bilgames turns to glory and renown as a mode of "immortality." With this in mind, he proposes to Enkidu a trip to the cedar Mountain. The doxology is "kal-ga dbil$_4$-ga-mes mi-dug-ga dnissaba za$_2$-mi" "Honor to the mighty god Bilgames, praise to the goddess Nissaba."[29]
	RELATION TO 7TH CENT. BCE AKKADIAN SBV OF GILGAMESH
	This poem has clearly been translated and included in SBV tablet V.
4) Bilgames and the Bull of Heaven	The incipit, and hence its title, is "šul-me$_3$-kam (Hero in Battle)."
	RELATION TO 7TH CENT. BCE AKKADIAN SBV OF GILGAMESH
	The Akkadian version of this in tablet VI represents an expansion of this Sumerian short poem.
5) The Death of Bilgames	This Sumerian poem is only partially preserved but it tells of the human quest for immortality, which is denied by the gods.
	RELATION TO 7TH CENT. BCE AKKADIAN SBV OF GILGAMESH
	In a sense the entire SBV version, especially tablets VII–VIII, represents an expansion of this poem's leitmotiv.
6) The Sumerian Flood	Although the Sumerian flood story does not refer to Gilgamesh or Bilgames, it does mention Ziusudra, the Sumerian Uta-napishti. The Sumerian flood story was adapted into the flood in Atra-ḫasis, although there were several versions of each concurrently.
	RELATION TO 7TH CENT. BCE AKKADIAN SBV OF GILGAMESH
	It is used in Tablet XI of Gilgamesh, but more aptly in the older epic Atra-ḫasis, from which epic Gilgamesh borrowed the flood story.

Geographically, fragments of the Gilgamesh epics spread from southern Iraq to northern modern Israel to the Hittite and Hurrian Mitanni Empires. (Turkey, Syria, and Northern Mesopotamia) from 2000–1200 BCE. Fragments were in Sumerian, Akkadian, Hurrian, and Hittite. In 1954, a shepherd discovered a fragment of the Gilgamesh Epic near the University of Chicago excavation dump in ancient Megiddo (modern Israel).[30] The scholar A. Westenholz would attribute this piece to the Middle Babylonian period (16th–15th centuries BCE, a dating which most modern scholars have espoused.

Fig. 8 - Typical broken, reassembled clay tablet fragment of the SVB of the Epic of Gilgamesh. Reverse side of Tablet V. Sulaymaniyah Museum. Source: https://dustoffthebible.com/blog-archive/2018/01/26/the-epic-of-gilgamesh-text-translation-tablets/.

6) OLD BABYLONIAN (2000–1600 BCE) EPICS OF GILGAMESH[31]

In the Old Babylonian period, there is evidence of several variable versions of a unified story of the exploits of Gilgameš. The idea that these were all fragments of one canonical "official" version is no longer maintained; rather some fragments seem to suggest several slightly varying forms of the epic; that indicates a tradition of the circulation of several orally-based versions.[37] The largest cuneiform of Gilgameš tablets are those of Philadelphia and of Yale (named from the museum collections that now hold them). Joined fragments from the library of King Ashurbanipal (669–627 BCE) in Nineveh yield at least one OB version. It seems to have the same plot as the SBV one-thousand year later. The ending of this OB version is missing. The flood story in this OB version seems much shorter than the SBV. It lacked the prologue of the SBV but included the famed carpe diem speech of Siduri, and the strange ending of tablet XII of the SBV. From catalogs of literary works, it seems to have been named after its incipit "šutur eli šarri" ("Surpassing all other Kings").

Outline of the Gilgamesh Epic (SBV)[33]

PROLOGUE: URUK
Gilgamesh (G.), the two-thirds divine king of Uruk,[34] is causing chaos in his city among the young men and women. The reasons are unclear but may be sexual with G.'s claiming the *jus primae noctis* from the brides or by constantly exhausting the young men with athletic contests. The exhausted citizens of Uruk petition the mother goddess Aruru to create an equal match for G. To keep him occupied and to afford them a respite.

ENKIDU OF THE STEPPES AND THE HARLOT ŠAMḪAT[35]		G.'S TWO DREAMS ABOUT ENKIDU
Enkidu (E.) is created as a hirsute wilding of the steppe (lullû).[36] He eats wild grasses and foods like his fellow animals; and slurps water as they do. He is described as a "murderous young man from the midst of the wilderness." A hunter discovers E. who releases all captive animals from his traps. The hunter reports his discovery to G., who dispatches a harlot Shamḫat to civilize him through sex: "E. was erect for 7 days!" She then feeds him "civilized foods": beer, bread, etc.[37] He becomes alienated from the animals of his prior primeval state. The narrator states, "He (E.) transitions from being a lullû to becoming like a man (amēlišime). Then Shamḫat tells E. about G.'s two dreams and leads him to Uruk to challenge G.	*Parallel Scenes*	G. tells his divine mother about this two dreams: 1. a meteor (kiṣru) from the sky (Anu). G. could not lift it; the men of Uruk stood around it and kissed its feet like a baby's. G. tells his mother Ninsun, "I loved it like a wife, and I caressed it." It was G.'s equal.[38] 2. an axe (ḫaṣṣinnu) was lying in the street of Uruk. Again G. brought it to Ninsun who responded: "My son the axe you saw is a man (amēlu)[39] you will love him like a wife and caress it; I shall make him your equal."

E. and G. meet and wrestle to no conclusive victory; nonetheless, they end by forming a pair of equals. There is a major textual gap; when the text resumes, the two now undertake what eventually will be two quest journeys, separated by a critical event.

TWO HEROIC EPIC JOURNEYS: 1.) ḤUMBABA & THE BULL OF HEAVEN & 2.) JOURNEY TO UT-NAPISHTI

ḤUMBABA

Against all advice, our two heroes set out to travel to the Cedar Forest (Lebanon), that the monster Ḥumbaba (older Ḥuwawa) guards. The text of tablet II of the SVB version describes the horrific guardian Ḥumbaba: "His voice is like the primeval deluge, his speech is fire, his breath is death, he can hear the faintest murmur in the forest for a distance of 60 leagues (ca. 315 miles away)." Despite mutual doubt, the two heroes arrive at the Cedar Mountain and the sun god equips them with the tools to overcome the ogre. After some hesitancy and the appeals of Ḥumbaba, they slay and behead him.

THE BULL OF HEAVEN

On their way back to Uruk, the goddess Ishtar tries to seduce G.; however, despite her attempts at blandishment, G. rudely mocks her by recalling her infidelity to her previous paramours. In the goddess's fury, she beseeches Anu to give her the majestic Bull of Heaven as an instrument of her peevishness. She even threatens Anu with her releasing the dead from the underworld. Ninsun appears on the walls of Uruk to denounce G. E. takes a leg from the slaughtered bull and slaps Ishtar with it. G. calls craftsmen who bejewel and gold plate the bull's horns for use as cornuate drinking vessels. That evening E. has a portentous nightmare, in which the gods meet, and Anu calls for the pair's death; however, Enlil confines lethal punishment just to E., who awakened recalls his ominous dream to G. Weeping, E. laments that in the underworld he will never again see his brother G. When E. learns his fate via dreams, he initially curses everybody who brought him to this point: Shamḫat and the hunter. The sun deity Shamash hears his grief and assuages E.'s torment by prophesying that G. will perform his brother's funereal ceremonies so prodigiously that the entire world will never forget E.'s renown. Now calmed, E. lies down to await his ineluctable fate. The extensive leave-takings between E. and G. are among the most moving in ancient literature. G. stays by his brother's now dead body for seven days until a maggot falls from E.'s nose.

G.'s anguish for the dead E. quickly turns to the realization of his own mortality, despite his partial divinity. His depression leads him to recall the one mortal (amēlu) who acquired divinity and immortality, Ut-Napishti, the Distant One,[40] who in his boat survived the Great Flood (Abūbu) by resting on the summit of Mount Mashu.

I shall die, so will I not be like E.?	a-na-ku a-mat-ma ul ki-i den-ki-du$_3$-ma-a
Grief has entered my heart.	ni-is-sa-a-tum i-te-ru-ub ina kar-ši-ia
I fear death so I roam the wilderness	mu-ta ap-lah$_3$-ma a-rap-pu-ud ṣēra (edin)
To the side of Uta-napishti the son of Ubara-Tutu.[41]	a-na le-et mUD-napišti (zi) mār (dumu) mubara-dtu-tu

G.'s journey takes him underneath the mountains in sheer darkness on the way Shamash travels from sunrise to sunset. Despite the inevitable obstacles that accompany this literary genre, e.g. two Scorpion-men guardians of the tunnel, our hero arrives at daylight by a sea. Thereupon, G. meets the alewife Suduri, who seeing him unkempt clad only in a shabby lionskin, runs home and bars her door. He eventually identifies himself and asks Siduri to show how he could cross the sea to the home of Uta-napishti. In the Old Babylonian version from Sippar, Suduri replies that since time immemorial nobody has crossed that sea of death; she counsels carpe diem, enjoy the moment rather than fighting our inevitable death.[42]

14'	sa-bi-tum a-na ša-a-šum iz-za-qar-am a-na ^{d}GIŠ[43]	The ale-wife spoke to him, to Gilgames:
iii 1	^{d}GIŠ e-eš ta-da-a-al	'O Gilgames, where are you wandering?
2	ba-la-ṭam$_2$ ša ta-sa-ah-hu-ru la tu-ut-ta	You cannot find the life that you seek:
3	i-nu-ma ilu (dingir)^{meš} ib-nu-u a-wi-lu-tam	when the gods created mankind,
4	mu-tam iš-ku-nu a-na a-wi-lu-tim	for mankind they established death,
5	ba-la-ṭam$_2$ i-na qa$_2$-ti-šu-nu iṣ-ṣa-ab-tu	life they kept for themselves.
6	at-ta ^{d}GIŠ hi ma-li ka-ra-aš-ka	You, Gilgames, let your belly be full,
7	ur-ri u$_3$ mu-ši hi-ta-ad-du$_2$ at-ta	keep enjoying yourself, day and night!
8	u$_4$-mi-ša-am šu-ku-un hi-du-tam	Every day make merry,
9	ur-ri u$_3$ mu-ši su-ur u$_3$ me-li-il	dance and play day and night!
10	lu ub-bu-bu ṣu -ba! (KU)-tu-ka	Let your clothes be clean!

11	qa₂-qa₂-ad-ka lu me-si me-e lu ra-am-ka-ta	Let your head be washed, may you be bathed in water!
12	ṣu₂-ub-bi ṣe-eḫ-ra-am ṣa-bi-tu qa₂-ti-ka	Gaze on the little one who holds your hand!
13	mar-ḫi-tum li-iḫ-ta- ad-da-a-am i-na su-ni-ka	Let a wife enjoy your repeated embrace!
14	an-na-ma ši-i[m-ti a-wi-lu-tim?]	Such is the destiny [of mortal men]

Nonetheless, Siduri suggests that he seek out Ur-shanabi, who is Uta-napishti's ferryman. Ur- shanabi reluctantly agrees to ferry him over to the flood-survivor's island provided G. can supply three hundred wooden poles, each of 30 meters' length. The voracious waters consume almost all the punting poles, but they finally land and meet Uta-napishti. He discards G.'s quest by reminding him:[44]

The Anunnaki, the great gods, were in assembly	da-nun-na-ki ilū (dinger)meš rabûtu (gal)meš paḫ-ru
Mamītum, the creator of fate, made a destiny with them,	dma-am-me-tum ba-na-at šim-ti itti (ki)-šu₂-nu ši-
They established death and life,	ma-tu₂ i-ši[m-ma]
(However), regarding death they did not reveal its day.	iš-tak-nu mu-ta u ba-la-ṭ[a]
	ša₂ mu-ti ul ud-du-u₂ ūmī (u₄)-šu

Uta-napishti recounts to G. how he—a mortal—achieved immortality and tells him of the flood and his survival. The flood account in tablet XI of the Gilgamesh Epic is borrowed from the flood in Atra-Ḫasis, the 18th-century BCE Babylonian Story of the Flood, where its presence is more germane, and hence primary. So, Uta-napishti's immortality resulted from a unique situation. The flood's survivor then challenges G. to stay awake for a week. Immediately the exhausted G. collapses into a deep slumber. To prove that the hero of Uruk could not stay awake, Uta-napishti asks his wife to bake a loaf of bread each day and place it next to G. After a week, G. awakens, but at once denies he slept, until Uta-napishti shows him the seven loaves of bread with their week-long advancing mold. G. is despondent: everywhere I turn is death! Thereupon, Uta- napishti instructs the boatman to take G. away and bathe him, shampoo him, and replace his clothing with regal attire. Uta-napishti's wife upbraids her husband for sending G. away empty- handed. So, Uta-napishti calls G. back and discloses to him a secret matter and mystery of the gods (amat niṣirti u parišti ša ilī): down on the sea floor is a thorned plant that rejuvenates. G. retrieves the plant and tells Ur-shanabi:

This plant is a plant for a crisis (?)	šam-mu an-nu šam-mu ni-kit-ti
By this means a man can arrive at vitality.[45]	ša₂ amēlu (lu₂) lib-bi-šu₂ i-kaš ša₂-du nap-šat(!)-su

EPILOGUE: URUK

G. began his return to Uruk. At thirty leagues, they made camp at a pool of water. G. went down into the water to clean himself; a snake smelled the plant and devoured it thereby gaining rejuvenation by shedding his skin. G. weeps at his loss and as they approach Uruk, G. tells Urshanabi to circumambulate the walls of Uruk and admire the brickwork. G.'s immortality shall rest in his walls around Uruk, as the proleptic Prologue had intimated.

Significance of SBV Gilgamesh Epic in the West

Many claims have been made for the impact of the Gilgamesh Epic on western literature: western Mediterranean littoral (Judaism, Aramaic literature), Greece, Syria, Latin and later literature. The eminent British Assyriologist Stephanie Dalley has argued for a Gilgamesh influence on many of the stories in 'Alf Layla wa-Laylah "One Thousand and One Nights" or "Arabian Nights," especially in the tales of Bulūqiyā. [46] Some would detect a G. echo/allusion in Siduri's recommendation (p. 15) in the Hebrew Bible book of Ecclesiastes (or aka Qoheleth):

> (Eccl. 9:7-9 NJB) So, eat your bread in joy, drink your wine with a glad heart, since God has already approved your actions. 8 At all times, dress in white and keep your head well scented. 9 Spend your life with the woman you love, all the days of futile life God gives you under the sun, throughout your futile days, since this is your lot in life and in the effort you expend under the sun.

A. R. George gives a cogent description and evaluation of such claims.[47] He is generally diffident in accepting these supposed allusions to G., since many so-called allusions are part of widely circulated common folk themes. There are similarities with Arabian Nights in the centuries-old formation of the two literary works. As a coverage of Gilgamesh in modernity, the student might consult Wikipedia's article on (https://en.wikipedia.org/wiki/Gilgamesh_in_ the_arts_and_popular_culture), which also has an extensive bibliography of modern works that are consciously imitative of Gilgamesh.

The Humanistic Nature of the Epic of Gilgamesh

The "Epic of Gilgamesh" explores several main timeless tenets of our humanity.

1. Our lives are riven by angst in face of our mortality, which we often try to assuage by by leaving behind a legacy, be it children or some personal equivalent of the "Walls of Uruk."

2. We, and certainly the British colonialism in the 19th century, are obsessed with the antomonies of culture (G.) versus the wild (Enkidu). When our sophisticated world teetered with the threats of Covid-19, many sought refuges in the wild of woods and sea.

3. The difference between reproduction and sexuality. The animals around wild Enkidu reproduce, he even suckled at their breasts; however, he must be specially introduced to human sexuality by the harlot (through which he becomes human)! His response to her is a seven day erection! We see that same dichotomy between reproduction and human sexuality in biblical Genesis. There the animals are male and female, but full sexuality involves human sexuality.

4. The role of homosexuality, the bro-romance between G. and E., whom G. loved as a wife. Here at last we can refer back to the puns on p. 32.

5. The importance of life as a journey of discovery. G. starts out as a spoiled, ego-centric brat but by his journeys and travails finally comes to accept his mortality and the walls of Uruk as his legacy.

Notes

[1] The importance of life as a journey of discovery. G. starts out as a spoiled, ego-centric brat but by his journeys and travails finally comes to accept his mortality and the walls of Uruk as his legacy. This reading of the cuneiform text and its translation is taken from Andrew George, who reads a slightly different Akkadian text: [ša₂ naq-ba i-mu-ru i]š-di ma-a-ti] and translates it as "[He who saw the Deep, the] foundation of the country." (The Babylonian Gilgamesh Epic: Introduction, Critical Edition and Cuneiform Texts. 2 vols. Vol. I. Oxford: Oxford University Press, 2003. 538–39; Vol. II (2003), pp.778. A book in the Ancient Near East employed its incipit as its title in ancient cuneiform literary catalogues, so the book Epic of Gilgamesh was called "ša₂ naq-ba i-mu-ru". Although much of the first line is in brackets, i.e., it is not preserved on any of the epic manuscripts, we can reconstruct the line from its title in cuneiform catalogues. Parpola, The Standard Babylonian Epic of Gilgamesh: Cuneiform Text, Transliteration, Glossary, Indices and Sign List. State Archives of Assyria Cuneiform Texts 1. 1997 reads:

ša₂ nag-ba i-mu-ru [lu-še]-ed-di ma-a-ti — Of him who found out all things I shall tell the lands

[ša₂ kul-la]-ti i-du-u₂ ka-la-[ma ḫa]-as-su — Of him who experienced everything I shall teach all.

The subscript numbers in Sumerian and Akkadian, e.g., the 4 in bil₄, designate to an Assyriologist the exact sign used in sign collections, since there are several cuneiform signs that were pronounced /bil/.

[2] Although I could provide my own translation, since this was the very first book I studied in Greek, however, my rendition could not compare to R. Fagles' masterful translation supplied here (Homer, The Odyssey. Tran. by R. Fagles and Introduction and Notes by B. Knox. Penguin Classics 70th Anniversary - Classic Journeys. New York: Penguin Books, 1999).

[3] W. Moran, "Ut-napishtim Revisited: Review of John Gardiner and John Maier, Gilgamesh and Robert Silverberg, Gilgamesh the King." New York Times Book Review, no. November 11, 1984 (1984): 13–14. For this reference and others by Moran, I am indebted to S. Ackerman's book When Heroes Love: The Ambiguity of Eros in the Stories of Gilgamesh and David. (Gender, Theory, and Religion. New York City: Columbia University Press, 2005), 246.

[4] W. Moran, "Rilke and the Gilgamesh Epic." JCS 32 (1980): 208–210.

[5] This probably refers to the 1911 literal translation of A. Ugnad, and H. Grossman, Das Gilgamesch-epos. Vol. 14, FRLANT. Göttingen: Vandenhoeck und Ruprecht, 1911.

[6] By "epic" is meant "a long narrative poem describing heroic events that happens over a period of time." A. R. George, The Babylonian Gilgamesh Epic, 3. They often involve interactions between gods and humans.

[7] The Sumerian king list: https://etcsl.orinst.ox.ac.uk/cgibin/etcsl.cgi?text=c.2.1.1&display=Crit&charenc=gcirc&lineid=c211.95#c211.95

[8] The dynasty of Ur III was particularly fond of B. because those kings regarded Uruk as their early predecessor. From this period on, B.'s name appears with a logograph of the Sumerian word diĝir (𒀭), designating the following name as a god. For B. as a god, see below.

[9] Sumerian King List iii 17–20. http:etcsl.orinst.ox.ac.uk/section2/tr211.htm.

[10] Kullab was one of the quarters that made up Uruk.

[11] The EN sign, not written here, is not part of the royal name, but probably a title meaning "Lord." The inscription is read from the left to right beginning with the sign resembling a capital "T" on its side.

[12] This inscription is from RIME E1.7.22.1.2; the drawing is from CDL P222739. Notice that the logogram for LUGAL (king) shows pictographically a man on his back wearing a crown.

[13] The pre-Sargonic kings ruled prior to Sargon of Akkad who founded a Semitic dynasty (as opposed to Sumerian) c. 24th–23rd centuries BCE.

[14] Also pronounced "Aga", /g/ and /k/ are similar velar plosives, however, /g/ is voiced (involving the vibration of the vocal cords). Notice the different pronunciations of initial /good/ and /king/.

[15] For the text see https://etcsl.orinst.ox.ac.uk/cgi-bin/etcsl.cgi?text=t.2.1.3#

[16] A colophon is a scribal note at the end of a cuneiform tablet telling something about the tablet and its scribe; it often contained the name of the monarch who had commissioned it.

[17] Translation is from A. R. George, The Babylonian Gilgames Epic (2003), 105. George reads the EN in king's name Enmebaraggesi as part of the name, rather than taking it as a title "lord."

[18] George, The Babylonian Gilgamesh Epic (2003), p. 127.

[19] Ibid., 128.

[20] These two deities are underworld gods; Ningishzida means "Lord of the Good Tree" whose roots descend to the underworld

[21] Lambert, W. G. "A Rare Exorcistic Fragment," in Riches Hidden in Secret Places: Ancient Near Eastern Studies in Memory of Thorkild Jacobsen (ed. Tzvi Abusch. Winona Lake: Eisenbrauns, 2002), 210.

[22] Delougaz, P., I. *Plano-Convex Bricks and the Methods of their Employment;II. The Treatment of Clay Tablets in the Field.* Edited by J. H. Breasted. Vol. 7, The Oriental Institute of the University of Chicago: Studies in Ancient Oriental Civilizations. Chicago: University of Chicago Press, 1933.

[23] There is no indication that these stories had been part of a larger inclusive Sumerian epic.

[24] A. R. George translates these Sumerian poems in *The Epic of Gilgamesh: The Babylonian Epic Poem and Other Texts in Akkadian and Sumerian* (New York: Barnes & Noble, 1999), pp. 141–208.

[25] Also known as "Gilgamesh, Enkidu, and the Netherworld."

[26] This is an informed guess about the meanings of gišellag and gišE.KID-ma. The determinative giš before a word tells us that the two items are made of "wood," the capital letters used in E.KID means we can identify the two cuneiform signs, but we are unsure of their value together as a digraph. The University of Pennsylvania Sumerian dictionary defines ellag as "a wooden ball;" However, for E.KID-ma, it only suggests "a wooden object used in a game."

[27] That is, XII:1 of the Epic of Gilgamesh is equivalent to line 172–of "Bilgames and the Netherworld" (aka Bilgames and the Ḫalub Tree).

[28] Also known as "Gilgamesh and the Land of the Living." There are several versions of this story.

[29] Nissaba was the goddess of writing.

[30] The University of Chicago excavated Megiddo (Tell al-Mutasallim) from 1925–1939. The Israel Museum labeled this fragment 55-2.

[31] King Hammurapi of Babylon (Hammurapi's law code) lived in the Old Babylonian period (OB).

[32] To us in the 21st century, the written seems the more important, the official version; however, in OB times the oral and the scribal were still quite active and cross affecting each other. Of course, we have trouble determining the exact roles the oral versions played since they do not survive.

[33] I regret that it is impossible to give line numbers for citations because the texts do not agree. The most authoritative numbering of the SBV is probably found in A. R. George, *The Babylonian Gilgamesh Epic: Introduction, Critical Edition and Cuneiform Texts*. 2 vols. Oxford: Oxford University Press, 2003. However, most readers will not have easy access to these two volumes.

[34] This was over three millennia before Mendelian genetics. Gilgamesh's father was the human king Lugalbanda; his mother was the goddess Ninsun.

[35] Shamḫat as a personal name that probably alludes to Akkadian shamḫatu "harlot."

[36] The Akkadian word "lullû" used of Enkidu means something like "pre-human." He is not yet a man (amēlu) "human."

[37] "Civilized" food is that which humans adapt from nature, so, for example, nature's grain is milled and becomes bread or beer.

[38] I shall discuss the sexual language here and in G.–Enkidu scenes later. I have given transliterations of the Akkadian here because they will play a key role in risqué puns discussed below.

[39] In the mouth of G.'s divine mother, "the lullû Enkidu becomes an amēlu 'a human.'"

[40] Mister "he saved his life" in Akkadian, which translates the Shuruppak hero Ziusudra in the Sumerian flood Story. In biblical Genesis, this equates of course to Noah.

[41] The Akkadian is from A. R. George, *The Babylonian Gilgamesh Story*, Tablet IX: 3–6. The translation is my own.

[42] The following quotation is taken from George, *The Babylonian Gilgamesh Epic* (2003), 278.

[43] At this time "Gilgamesh" was abbreviated to dGIŠ.

[44] Ibid, Tablet X: 319–322.

[45] The name "Gilgamesh" probably means "an ancestor (bilga) becomes young (mes)."

[46] Stephanie Dalley, "Gilgamesh in the Arabian Nights." JRAS ns 1 (1991): 1–17; Ibid., "The Tale of Bulūqiyā and the 'Alexander Romance' in Jewish and Sufi Mystical Circles," in *Tracing the Threads: Studies in the Vitality of Jewish Pseudepigrapha* (Early Judaism and Its Literature) (ed. J. C. Reeves. Atlanta: Scholars Press, 1994), 239–269.

[47] George, *The Babylonian Gilgamesh Epic* (2003), 54–70.

Burney Relief, also known as "Queen of the Night." High-relief terracotta panel, 49.5 cm high. Originally colored. Southern Mesopotamia, 1800-1750 BCE, exact provenance unknown. British Museum, Object no. 2003,0718.1. Drawing by Cheryl De Ciantis.

The Goddess Would Like a Word

By Cheryl De Ciantis

*She stirs confusion and chaos against those who are disobedient to her,
speeding carnage and inciting the devastating flood.[1]*

With her, the desert is filled with a glorious garden![2]

The goddess Ishtar[3] is the oldest goddess we know from extant written
evidence, in the form of cuneiform tablets from Mesopotamia, created
beginning nearly 5,000 years ago in Uruk, the chief city of the early Sumerian
dynastic empire.[4] The Sumerians, Akkadians, Babylonians and Assyrians all
revered Ishtar as the goddess of love and of war. She was recognized as by far
the most powerful female deity among the inter-related deities of the
Mesopotamian pantheons, often surpassing her father and brother gods in the
scope of her accomplishments. Her name appears more often in Sumerian
myths than any other deity.[5]

For all her ancient fame, the goddess is vastly distant from us in time and
space. As the Mesopotamian politico-cultural powers waned, their material
remains largely disappeared and remained mute to our understanding until
the late 19th century. The stories that arose out of the Mesopotamian religious
imagination were buried for nearly two millennia, and Ishtar vanished from
the Western consciousness.

The Pantheon: Hierarchy and Order

By contrast, history never lost sight of the Greek gods and goddesses.
Their characterizations, by Homer and Hesiod (c. 8th and 7th cent. BCE
respectively) are what most of us in the primarily European-influenced
cultural domains recall when we think of "myth," which is, after all, a Greek
word. The Greek gods we are so familiar with are part of a pantheon, a mythic
structure common across many mythologies whose gods have familial
connections to each other, and are ruled by, most typically, a father sky-god.

In Greek mythology it is Zeus, who wields cosmic thunderbolts. The
Greek myths exemplify a patriarchal hierarchy that is familiar to us—some
gods are expected to be more powerful and authoritative than others, and
some are seen as secondary figures, ruled by the ruler. For example, Hera,

more often than not unwillingly, is subject to the authority of her brother-husband Zeus. The divine children of Zeus (not all children of gods are immortal) have their own roles, duties, domains of influence and privileges. Figures like local nature divinities such as "nymphs" occupy a lower status. The familial pantheon with hierarchically distributed authority is an image that lies at the core of many of our cultural beliefs and expectations (and consequently, our own social norms and behaviors).

The Mesopotamian gods and goddesses were also represented as a familial hierarchy under various names. In the Epic of Gilgamesh, the father, storm and sky god is Enlil. Brother and sister Shamash and Ishtar are Enlil's children. Anu is the creator-god. Neither Zeus nor Enlil are creator-gods, rather they oversee and sustain the order of creation—it is also common in myth for creator-gods or -goddesses to withdraw to a more abstract dimension once their work is done, a role that was named *deus absconditus* by medieval Christian theologians. However, the Yahweh of Genesis still walked embodied in the evening time, greeting Abraham and Sarah in the oak grove, and Anu is still present to the mythic characters of the Epic of Gilgamesh.

Mortal kings were accorded a lineage of direct descent from gods or goddesses, or were symbolically married to a deity, legitimizing their role and the status of their people within an ordered cosmos. This is a persistent theme in myth and survived well into modern times as the "divine right of kings," as a means of legitimization of dynasties and attributing a mandate to their actions which superseded human law. One of the original jobs of bards—the earliest were often regarded themselves as semi-divine—was to sing not only the deeds but the genealogies of kings and heroes, for example the lengthy catalogue of "begots" in Genesis of the Hebrew Bible. The administratively minded Mesopotamians recorded successive King Lists containing both historical and legendary kings over centuries.

Interpretive Lenses, Enduring Assumptions

A significant influence on our preconceptions and expectations about the most ancient stories comes from European Biblical scholars, especially the sincere Christians whose project over the last few centuries has been to attempt to prove the historical veracity of the Bible. When the Epic of Gilgamesh first came to light its tale of a primordial Flood and a Noah-like figure aroused great excitement. Ethnography, which rose as an aspiring scientific field of study in the 19th century, contributed to the layers of interpretive bias by offering carefully categorized rationales to explain the lifeways and practices of indigenous and ancient peoples. Possibly the single most influential of these was Sir James George Frazer, author of *The Golden Bough,* first published in 1890. Frazer posited that humans developed—meaning morally and ethically —from more primary, primitive beliefs and practices based in supplicatory ritual and sympathetic magic, to organized religion, to the intellectual pinnacle of science; and that religion itself arose out of fertility rites and the sacrifice, whether ritually or actually, of the old king whose role was duly invigorated by the next in line, generally at the dark of the year in a seasonal/ cyclical pattern reflecting the movements of the cosmos observable to all since the dawn of time. One of the enduring effects of Frazer's work, though ethnologists have rejected his thesis for lacking evidence, is that female deities are still seen in the imagination of many primarily as dynastic guarantors through reproduction and emblems of fertility and consequential maternal care (of their own children or of earthly abundance). This also means that roles which do not issue in offspring or center in nurturance require a different categorization, for example, The Harlot.

More recent observations, based on new archaeological evidence, new technologies, and voices newly admitted to the academy and our avenues of discourse continue to shift our understandings of ancient figures. The Goddess as idea was invested with new social and political meanings with the rise of second wave feminism, which popularized the "feminine face of god," an encouragement to women seeking a more positive and empowering gender identity than helpmeet, housewife and passive sex-object. At the same time aspects of this movement, amplifying Romantic-era European speculations about feminine power, contributed to an overestimation of possible evidence suggesting a supposed all-powerful pre-patriarchal Great Goddess, which itself is undergoing evaluation of available data.[6] But in coming to terms with the huge difficulties in understanding the complexities of ancient minds, in many ways different but no less sophisticated than our own, we benefit from increasingly diverse voices in the scholarly community as well as the community of writers and artists pursuing evidential and imaginal renderings which show us ways to question even our most cherished assumptions.

Ishtar: Goddess of Love and War

Lest we lose sight of her again, let's return to Ishtar. She was not known for her patience.

She was revered as a goddess of both love and war; tales that were devoted to both her acts of vigorous and joyous sensuality and vividly explicit sexuality, as well as to her fierce and frequent acts of violence are hugely significant parts of the earliest literature we have inherited. Very possibly her seemingly contradictory and changing nature sometimes puzzled her devotees through the millennia of her mythic ascendance in ancient Mesopotamia and into the wider Middle East and eastern Mediterranean. More to the point: how are we today to understand a goddess of both love and war?

Ishtar the Lover

Beautiful, youthful, affectionate, enthusiastic, assertive and voluble, Ishtar is the goddess of love. We may be reminded of one of her mythic/syncretic derivatives, Greek Aphrodite, though many have forgotten that she, like Ishtar, is the goddess of white doves not only by reason of their soft, cooing attraction, but also by reason of their persistent dedication to mating. Both are goddesses who indulge in and who by example exalt and inspire physical intercourse.[7] Among the temple offerings made to Ishtar, many were in the form of a vulva.[8] The purposes of their donors may have ranged from praise offerings to the goddess identified with human sexuality and nature's flourishing, to acknowledgment of the goddess's symbolic legitimizing relation to the dynastic king and his city, to specific expressions of gratitude or pleas for success in sexual relations.

Ishtar uses her words and is exceptionally specific about her desires and expectations of sex. In the traditions of Mesopotamian love-poetry featuring the goddess, she is depicted as anticipating the joys of marriage or newly wed, celebrating the joy and excitement of sexuality in direct language. Ishtar's love for Dumuzi is celebrated in poetry. They are young, they are in love and Ishtar fantasizes about lovemaking and the joys of marriage.[9]

See now, our breasts stand out; see now, hair has grown on our genitals, signifying my progress to the embrace of a man![10]
Let us be very glad about my genitals! Dance, dance! Later on it will delight him, it will delight him![11]

Your coming here is life indeed, your entering our house is abundance; lying by your side is my utmost joy. My sweet, let us delight ourselves on the bed.[12]

A number of scholars note that the love-poetry of Ishtar mentions anticipation of "ploughing" as a metaphor of penetrative intercourse, but also of anticipatory wetness, and strong suggestions of thrilling orgasm.[13] She also uses her words to set out the required qualifications of her lover, as well as terms of consent.

Procreation, however, is not primary among Ishtar's functions as a love-goddess (nor was it for Aphrodite, who, myths tell us, bore children, but mythic accounts are not devoted to her nurturance of them). Ishtar is not characterized as a mother, and maternal functions like breastfeeding and midwifery are overseen by other female divinities.[14]

Ishtar the Daughter, Ishtar the Sister

The impetuous young Ishtar longing for sexual satisfaction also has clear connotations of relational belonging and her family shows interest in the conjugal happiness of their daughter and sister. Ishtar and her family members verbalize their ties of affectionate intimacy and support, and the connection between Ishtar and her brother Utu/Shamash is especially clear. Ishtar and Shamash share a special affection; he prepares with lavish care and aesthetic consideration the bed on which she will receive Dumuzi. Her mother Ningal too expresses affirmation toward Ishtar's chosen spouse Dumuzi, and Ishtar affirms her gratitude for the guidance and protection her mother shows to the young goddess about to cross the threshold of adulthood and sexual maturation.

As Pryke points out, "The emphasis on pleasure and intimacy, rather than pure sex, in texts related to the goddess has been largely overlooked in modern scholarship...."[15] Though Ishtar can be highly contentious and competitive with her close connections, the significance of family inter-relations, power interdependencies and demonstrated affection in many of the stories of Ishtar and other Mesopotamian deities stand in contrast to myths depicting the familial relations of the Greek gods, which are more often characterized by intra-familial contention than caring and sharing.

Ishtar the Transgressor

> I have given the cult-players their daggers and goads
> I have given the singers of laments their drums and tambours
> I have changed the sex of the cult impersonators.[16]

A very different side of Ishtar is expressed in her ancient reputation as a gender-bender capable of changing the sex of her followers, or her enemies, in certain situations which may have been seen by some as transgressive and potentially threatening or dangerous in her time; and was viewed with scant sympathy in more recent times. Lately a more diverse scholarly view has come to be articulated that raises questions about the many meanings and attributions of gender; as well as of literary intentions and devices (including satire and irony) in the context of poems and epics.

A persistent shadow aspect of Ishtar's modern reputation lies in the cultural assumptions and prejudices leading to the "historiographical myth" of temple prostitution. There is very little suggestion in actual textual evidence that merits the term prostitution, particularly with regard to the modern imputation of degraded status, or the implication that sex was exchanged for material gain and that it anciently received religious sanctioning. The meanings attributed to the "concept of a potential ritual enactment [of] divine marriage between Ishtar (and a representative, either in human form or a statue) and a Mesopotamian king is one that has captured scholarly attention like few other aspects of her goddess image."[17] The tendency to literalize scant evidence toward modern preconceptions and fantasies ignored the possible meanings of sexuality and sacrality in the ancient world.

What has also confused modern observers is that it appears that the normative expectations of sexuality on the part of Mesopotamians can be characterized as uniquely fluid. This does not mean that social structures such as marriage were meaningless. It has been long noted by scholars that Mesopotamian gods and goddesses served functions that might seem counter-intuitive to us, for example the evidence that multiple goddesses performed administrative roles that were not restricted to activities we might think of as masculine or oriented exclusively to female interests and welfare but served the entire community. Husband-and-wife divine pairs were commonly known, showing the importance of marriage; yet these figures also exchanged sex and function over time in stories and god-lists, suggesting that many divine roles and functions were gender-neutral.

Gilgamesh and Enkidu share a love that would be considered by many to be transgressive—certainly we have not resolved issues around gender, sexuality and identity, which remain enormous challenges to our own era with huge societal ramifications. What might have been more astonishing to the people who first encountered their story was that Gilgamesh repudiated the offered love of Ishtar, and repudiated the established tradition of kingly legitimation that would have come from the goddess's offer of marriage. It is perhaps not possible for us to discern the original meanings embedded in this text. Readers in modern times also attributed a negatively transgressive meaning to Shamhat's role (the "temple prostitute," "The Harlot") in humanizing the wild man Enkidu through protracted coitus and cast a blind eye on Shamhat's other teachings (which perhaps, penetrated once she had Enkidu's undivided attention?). On the other hand, many European readers in recent centuries would not have found the civilizing touch of a courtesan to be at all a far-fetched idea.[18] It may be reasonable for us to consider whether Shamhat's role might be an example that expresses the civilizing significance of the sexual powers of Ishtar as tutelary goddess.

Ishtar the Vengeful, Ishtar the Destroyer

My lady confronted the mountain range.
She advanced step by step.
She sharpened both edges of her dagger.
She grabbed Ebih's neck as if ripping up esparto grass.
She pressed the dagger's teeth into its interior.
She roared like thunder.[19]

Because the mountain Ebih arrogantly refuses to bow to her power, Ishtar destroys it, "roaring like thunder." She is a storm goddess, capable of filling the sky, relentless in vengeance and she is famed for her indomitable strength. This is one of her more famous exploits. Ishtar's violence was celebrated and feared. As the goddess of both love and war, she was invincible.

When Gilgamesh criticizes Ishtar for her treatment of her lovers, he likely refers to two well-known stories about the goddess: her descent into the Underworld and her return whereupon her husband Dumuzi is forced to take her place to fill the empty space in the realm of the dead; and her pursuit and annihilation of Sukaletuda the shepherd.

Love-poetry celebrated Ishtar and Dumuzi's mutual longing and sexual delight in marriage, as well as remarking on Dumuzi's own beauty and charm, and his suitability as ardent husband to the breathless goddess. In the version of Inanna/Ishtar's descent to the Underworld that we are most familiar with, Ishtar miraculously and unexpectedly returns to find that Dumuzi has not sufficiently mourned her death, and points to him as the substitute who must take her place in the Underworld realm of her sister Ereshkigal. In other versions, it is not Dumuzi who is substituted, but who remains as the semi-divine king whose association with the goddess legitimizes his rule. However the stories end, Ishtar laments the death of Dumuzi even when she is responsible for it.[20]

The tale of Inanna and Sukaletuda (c.1800 BCE) tells of Ishtar's rape by the shepherd Sukaletuda who finds her asleep under a tree, exhausted after her cosmic travels. She awakes to find herself violated but does not know the identity of her assailant. The goddess of sex can be raped; there are and always have been limits to what is permissible and what requires redress or vengeance. It is the goddess who is accustomed to choosing her sexual partners and awards them with her positive regard and favors; she is female but she is not free for the taking. Fleeing her rage, Sukaletuda has taken his father's advice and hidden in the cities. But still fearful he flees to the mountains. Unable to find him, Ishtar uses one of her divine powers, her ME, to expand to cosmic size, stretching across the entire sky to search him out. When she finds him, she destroys him.[21]

Does Gilgamesh get these stories wrong? Or does he get them right?

Ishtar of the Powerful ME

The heavens are mine and the earth is mine: I am heroic! [....]
Which god compares with me?[22]

Among Ishtar's most salient qualities is the amount of energy she invests in gathering status and power. This she accrues through seeking or importuning gifts and privileges from her father, Enlil, and from her many conquests and assaults on other divinities or figures of power to add to her own.

The ME are the divine powers accorded to Mesopotamian gods. We are accustomed to the idea that various god/desses served unique functions. The practical and administratively-minded Mesopotamians conceived these functions as material and political privileges, emblems of authority, and/or competence, and often as objects. Their gathering is attributed to Enlil, and to

Enki their subsequent distribution among the divinities. The local divinities retained the greatest for themselves then distributed others to their kings, clients and supplicants. A large list of the ME ranged from "EN-ship," the political power of a priestess, to professional designations such as blacksmith, to natural phenomena like flood, to objects such as regalia denoting royal authority (scepter, insignia), to weapons, specific musical instruments, to craft skills and implements—not necessarily in order of any precedence or priority we might assume by our standards to be rational. There are also negative ME such as "troubled heart."[23]

Ishtar's first appearance is as the city-patron of Uruk. The Bronze Age Mediterranean and Near and Middle East held traditions of a "citadel goddess" who was honored as the divine representative of power and protection in the fortified, wealthy city states (think of Uruk and its famous walls, legendarily erected by Gilgamesh) that characterized the period before the catastrophic Late Bronze Age Collapse of political, economic and likely environmental disaster, and widespread warfare and destruction, c. 1200 BCE, which was followed by a "dark age."[24] The citadel goddess also represented the authority of the king and the shared identity and pride of the city's people. In Uruk, this was Ishtar. In Argos in pre-Hellenic Peloponnese Greece this was Hera, who independently functioned as such many centuries before the mythic and political elevation of Zeus. Uruk thrives on the ME that Ishtar brings.

The first named author to compose hymns to Inanna/Ishtar and the first poet known to history by name is Enheduanna (23rd cent. BCE), a priestess of the moon god Nanna in Ur. She was the daughter of Sargon, founder of the Akkadian empire and her post in Ur may have been a diplomatic move to foster harmony between the Sumerian religion and the Akkadian.[25] The poet praises the goddess "for her beauty, her ferocity, and her powerful voice, as well as for the close bonds she shares with her fellow deities, and her ability to wield the divine powers of the ME:

> Praise be to the destroyer of foreign lands, endowed with the divine powers by An[u] [the Mesopotamian creator-god], to my lady enveloped in beauty...."[26]

The ME represent status not nature—they can be traded or lost to other divinities; or stolen as Ishtar does. Yet Ishtar's beauty, energy and "voice" represent her uniquely feminine and effective power.[27]

Ishtar the Transcendent

The story of Ishtar best known today is the tale of her journey to the Underworld. The objective would be to gain powers for herself that were the domain of her sister Ereshkigal and thereby further elevate her own cosmic status. Ishtar prepares by applying her cosmetics and dressing herself with care. She brings with her the seven most important ME she has achieved. She instructs her nurse/adjutant Ninshubar in a strategy of mourning protocol for the dead and the family gods she must plead with if she needs rescue from the world of the dead.

> Father Enki, the lord of great wisdom, knows about the life-giving plant and the life-giving water. He is the one who will restore me to life.[28]

Arrayed for her project with the raiment and jewels embodying her seven ME, Ishtar bangs on the first of the seven gates of the Underworld. Her sister Ereshkigal instructs the gatekeeper to bolt the seven gates and admit Ishtar through one at a time, stripping her of another item among her clothes and jewels, representing her ME, at each gate. When, on reaching Ereshkigal's throne, naked Ishtar seats herself on it. The judges of Death convict her for her transgression and Ishtar dies. Her corpse is hung from a hook. At her death, all earthly fertility ceases and the people in the city above lament loudly. Ninshubar duly calls on the gods. All but Enki refuse. Enki's emissary (or two emissaries created by Enki who may be sexless) charmingly gains the assent of Ereshkigal and is permitted to carry Ishtar's corpse back to the daylight world. Returning through the seven gates Ishtar is able to retrieve each of the seven items that represent her ME.[29]

Once Ishtar is released from death, a substitute must be provided. Ishtar will not accept the offers of sacrifice of those loyal to her. But then she sees Dumuzi. She has shared enthusiastic sexual bliss with him, legitimized him through marriage. Now, to her eyes he displays no grief for her and she points the finger. He is carried to the Underworld in her place.

Ishtar's journey to the Underworld is the first in literature and unique. For example, Odysseus and Orpheus both find sanctioned safeguards for their transgression into the dread territory—and their quests are not bids for power but bids for love and neither suffers death. Ishtar has gained ME in her return from the Underworld. When in the Epic of Gilgamesh she threatens to call out the dead to overwhelm the living in revenge for the slaying of the Bull of Heaven, which she herself has called forth, it is no idle threat. It is rather a threat on the scale of weapons of mass destruction, issued by someone whose finger is firmly, and thanks to her ME, legally on the button.

The Politics of Mythopoesis

It is easy to assume that the stories we have received from the ancients are immutable. From them we freely create our own renewed works of art and entertainment. And myths that do not speak to us sufficiently to inspire us to renew and reinterpret them do not remain alive. Joseph Campbell listed several of the functions of myth; two of them are especially important: myths serve to preserve cultural norms and traditions, and new myths arise when hearts and mind change.[30] These may sound like mutually exclusive operations but they are forever cycling in complementary rhythms in human time and mind.

Mythopoeisis was a term coined in the 19th century from two Greek words, mythos (myth, originally from *muthos*, mouth) and *poiesis* (making, creating). [31] When we recycle old stories or create stories that feel new (such as Mary Shelley's Frankenstein in the early 19th century and science fiction starting in the late 19th) we are engaging in mythopoesis.[32] What we create in the age of artificial intelligence is just beginning to reveal itself but will inevitably contain germs of the myths that originated with our species (another word for this is archetype).

What may come as a surprise to some is that the ancients had not only religious and artistic but political intentions and goals in creating and amplifying stories. By the time of the earliest writing, mythic stories were already old, already told and retold with breathtaking mnemonic and improvisational artistry.[33] Homer tells of the god of craft, Hephaistos, creating robots "with strength and voice" and Hesiod tells of his creation of Pandora, the first flesh and blood woman, also with "strength and voice" and certainly one of the earlier literary examples of biotechnology. The tales Homer told of the goddess Hera, among others, are subject now to re-examination with regard to how recognizable memes from older stories and trans- missions were mytho-poeticized into new forms. In the case of the *Iliad*, its commitment to written form and subsequent dissemination served at least in part the project of unifying the heterogeneous cultural domains of archaic Greece into a social/political/economic unity known as the Pan-Hellenization (beginning around the 8th cent. BCE and the first instance of written Greek). Hera, who is mythopoeticized by Homer into a shrewish wife, like Ishtar was once revered as an independent citadel goddess of great power and renown far beyond the boundaries of her seat in Argos; as, similarly, Ishtar's renown expanded far beyond her original seat in Uruk.

That ancient stories, even creation stories, may have expressed sophisticated minds seems to many of us a transgressive idea, nearly unimaginable. Yet we have always been human, with much the same wetware, much the same brain-functioning, for the lifespan of our species so far. While certain of our ways of thinking and being have changed, and more change is to come, as humans we still see what we expect to see; we create what we want others to see. This is in one context propaganda; in another, art. There are many times that they have been known to overlap. And to keep echoing.

Even the poem telling the story of Ishtar's rape tells too of her act of mercy, to us likely strange, in preserving Sukaletuda's name so that he will not entirely perish to memory. The Greek concept of kleos, fame, is similar: it preserves the names and renown of heroes to outlast their deaths. Achilles, the rageful and wantonly destructive hero of the Iliad, the "man of wrath," has a divine mother but even she cannot prevent his mortal death. Like Achilles, Gilgamesh will meet a mortal end, but will live in art for eternity. Too, though its nature is not described in specifically coital terms in either case, we may consider the love between Achilles and Patrokles in the Iliad as a possible echo of the love between Gilgamesh and Enkidu. The death of Patrokles unleashes both Achilles' towering grief and monstrous rage and propels him back into the fight against the Trojans.

What we are to make of all of these stories, and more, is up to us.

NOTES

[1] *Inana C*, ETCSL (Electronic Text Corpus of Sumerian Literature) 4.07.3 (quoted in Pryke, 48). In this essay, I will make substantial use of Louise Pryke's excellent book *Ishtar* (Routledge, 2017). Pryke's book is part of the excellent series Gods and Heroes of the Ancient World; Series Editor, Susan Deacy. Also recommended for further study: Asher-Greve, Julia and Joan Goodnick Westenholz, *Goddesses in Context: On Divine Powers, Roles, Relationships and Gender in Mesopotamian Textual and Visual Sources* (Academic Press Fribourg, 2013). Internet Archive: https://archive.org/details/AsherGreveWestenholz2013GoddessesInContext/page/n249/mode/2up

[2] Dumuzid-Inana P, ETCSL 4.08.16 (quoted in Pryke, 64).

[3] Also known in the oldest documented sources as Inanna from nin-an-na, "Lady of Heaven," the names Ishtar and Inana or Inanna are taken to denote the same goddess (Pryke, 6).

[4] Knowledge of cuneiform was lost to history until discoveries led to its gradual decipherment starting in the 1850s. 20 new lines from the Epic of Gilgamesh were recovered (some from looters in Iraq) and translated in 2011. See: https://www.openculture.com/2015/10/20-new-lines-from-the-epic-of-gilgamesh-discovered-in-iraq-adding-new-dimensions-to-the-story.html. AI is now being used to assist in identification and translation. See: https://www.biblicalarchaeology.org/daily/archaeology-today/ai-unlocks-ancient-texts/

[5] The folklorist and storyteller Diane Wolkstein in collaboration with the Assyriologist Samuel Noah Kramer brought Inanna/Ishtar to the attention of contemporary readers with their book *Inanna, Queen of Heaven and Earth: Her stories and hymns from Sumer* (Harper & Row, 1983).

[6] Johan Jakob Bachofen's theory of *Mutterrecht* (in English, *Mother Right: an investigation of the religious and juridical character of matriarchy in the Ancient World*, 1861), asserted that society and culture arose out of a prehistoric maternal ur-religion that was ultimately replaced by the paternalistic structures that still dominate most societies, was a major influence on scholars and artists. This view helped to fuel the Goddess Movement starting in the late 1960s, in part as a corrective to the misogyny many have seen as characterizing the monotheisms. The rising prominence of intersectionality as a scholarly method for analyzing power dynamics has led to greater attention to ethnicity, sexuality, gender and the evidence of oppression and domination as key factors in understanding history.

[7] Aphrodite's origin myth tells of her generation from the semen emitted from the severed phallus of Ouranos which fell from the heavens into the ocean when the primordial Titan was castrated by his son Kronos (who in turn was overthrown by his son Zeus). Homer depicts Aphrodite as a daughter of Zeus, but the older version highlights her generational precedence and more primordial nature as a of goddess of lust (who mated with Ares, the Greek god of war)—and casts a suggestive light on Aphrodite's possible inheritance of certain of Ishtar's characteristics.

[8] Pryke, 56.

[9] In this, we may see the origin of the ecstatic love poetry of the Biblical Song of Songs.

[10] *Dumuzid-Inanna C*, ETCSL 4.08.3 (quoted in Pryke, 35).

[11] *Dumuzid-Inanna C*, ETCSL 4.08.3 (quoted in Pryke, 43).

[12] *Dumuzid-Inanna G*, ETCSL 4.08.07 (quoted in Pryke, 44).

[13] Pryke, 45.

[14] Likewise, "Scholars have noted that, while the scope of Ishtar's identity is wide-ranging, she is never depicted as old" (Pryke, 109).

[15] As Pryke points out, "The emphasis on pleasure and intimacy, rather than pure sex, in texts related to the goddess has been largely overlooked in modern scholarship" (24).

[16] Inanna and Ebih, Foster, Benjamin R. *The Age of Agade: Inventing Empire in Ancient Mesopotamia* (Abingdon: Routledge, 2015), 346-347.

[17] It must be noted that the idea of temple prostitution originated in antiquity in the writings of Herodotus, and even then represented a cultural prejudice. "Although it was once widely accepted in scholarship that the practice of temple prostitution originated in the Ancient Near East, there are no known texts from Ancient Near Eastern sources which reference this." See Pryke 20-23; see also analysis by Beard, Mary and John Henderson, "With This Body I Thee Worship: Sacred Prostitution in Antiquity," *Gender and History* 9 (1997), 480-503; on distortions in interpretation of historical evidence or lack thereof, and categories of sexual intercourse in sacred contexts that may be derived from ancient sources see also: Budin, Stephanie, *The Myth of Sacred Prostitution in Antiquity* (New York: Cambridge University Press, 2008).

[18] Examples include Veronica Franco, a 16th century Venetian *cortigiana onesta* renowned for her poetry, philanthropy, advocacy and political acumen as an adviser to her clients and others. The term distinguished sex workers who were celebrated not only for their beauty but also for their intellect and influence in society and who were able to accrue and manage significant wealth (as distinct from the "streetwalker" or *cortigiana di lume*, whose class-status and poverty restricted them to transactional sex-work or to trafficking). See: Wikipedia: "Courtesan" for a list of renowned courtesans from diverse cultures and historical eras.

[19] *Inanna and Ebih* in Black, J.A., Cunningham, G., Robson, E., and Zólyomi, G. *The Electronic Text Corpus of Sumerian Literature*, (Oxford, 1998), 138-143. https://www.mesopotamiangods.com/inanna-and-ebih/

[20] Pryke, 42.

[21] Partial text of Inanna and Su-kale-tuda (c. 1800 BCE) can be found here: https://www.worldhistory.org/article/2127/inanna-and-su-kale-tuda/

[22] *Hymn to Inana, F* 21-33, ETCSL 4.07.6 (quoted in Asher-Greve and Westenholz, 76).

[23] For a list of the ME see Kramer, Samuel Noah, *The Sumerians: Their History, Culture, and Character* (Chicago: University of Chicago Press, 1963),116.

[24] There is substantial evidence for the Late Bronze Age Collapse of established states in the wide region surrounding the Eastern Mediterranean and Near East, the causes of which may have varied in different areas and likely reflected already developing vulnerabilities ranging from climate change, plant diseases and rising food shortage, to invasion, to entrenched dependence on copper amid the innovation of ironworking in the Hittite Empire (c. 1380 BCE). See Cline, Eric H., *1177 B.C.: The Year Civilization Collapsed* (Princeton University Press, 2014). The kingdom of Ugarit in modern northern coastal Syria, occupied as early as the 8th millennium BCE, disappeared completely, its population dispersed. Its gigantic library of cuneiform tablets was rediscovered in 1928, and the epic Baal Cycle came to light (composed c. 1500–1300 BCE). The Ugaritic god Baal is mentioned in the Hebrew Bible; and the epic likely contributed to the origins of Greek gods as later depicted by Homer, such as Hephaistos the god of metallurgy, arts and architecture, possibly inspired by

the Ugaritic smith-god Kothar-wa-Hasis. Scenes in *Iliad* Book 18 appear to have been inspired by the Baal text. See De Ciantis, Cheryl, *The Return of Hephaistos: Reconstructing the Fragmented Mythos of the Makers* (Tucson: Kairios Press, 2018), 150-153.

[25] "An interesting parallel to Enheduanna is provided by the Greek poet Sappho, who wrote over 1500 years later. Like Sappho, Enheduanna's compositions focused on a love goddess [Aphrodite]" Pryke, 17.

[26] *Inana B*, ETCSL 4.07.2 (quoted in Pryke, 17).

[27] In the writings of both Homer and Hesiod, the specific epithet of having "voice and strength" is attributed to female characters which include Hephaistos's creations of the beautiful female forge assistants he crafted from gold—among the earliest robots depicted in ancient literature; and Pandora, the first mortal woman, fashioned from clay by Hephaistos at the behest of Zeus. The epithet denotes high intelligence and fully independent agency. See De Ciantis, 48-49 and 117-118.

[28] *Inanna's Descent to the Netherworld*, ETCSL 1.4.1 (quoted in Pryke, 102).

[29] Pryke suggests that The Burney Relief (frontispiece illustration accompanying this essay) can be assumed to represent Ishtar. She is often depicted accompanied by or standing on the backs of lions; her raptor-feet suggest her deadly fierceness (as does her iconographic connection with the giant scorpions she defeated in her quest to overthrow An). The owls are a symbol of night/dark powers and recall Ishtar's association with not only the planet Venus as the morning star (similarly to Aphrodite/Venus) but also as the evening star, which, heralding night, is gendered as male in other mythologies. Ishtar's identification with both may also be a contributor to her ancient reputation as gender-bending. For more details on Ishtar's iconography in Mesopotamian art and literature, see Pryke, Chapter 6.

[30] On functions of myth and mythopoesis, see De Ciantis, 22-26.

[31] Doty, William G. *Mythography: The Study of Myths and Rituals.* 2nd. ed. (Tuscaloosa: University of Alabama Press, 2000), 11.

[32] See: Baldick, Chris, *In Frankenstein's Shadow: Myth, Monstrosity, and Nineteenth-century Writing* (Oxford: Clarendon, 1987).

[33] For the development and transmission of pre-literate, oral bardic composition, leading to the Homeric epics and other literary works, see Lord, Albert, *The Singer of Tales* (Cambridge: Harvard University Press, 1960).

GILGAMESH CON/QUEST
The epic dramatized in seven scenes

PROLOGUE

The play begins in the lobby. The actors create a large wedding scene with dancing, music and singing. MUSIC: "Prologue - Wedding Song No. 1." There is a procession around the space where actors and audience join in celebrating the marriage of a young couple. An old man circulates among the guests (both actors and audience), claiming to be Gilgamesh. He is in fact Gilgamesh returning to Uruk from his long journey, but no one believes him.

GUEST:
> It is time for celebration!

Rest of the chorus join in singing the wedding song. MUSIC: "Dance, Dance, Dance."

> Dance, dance, dance
> With the wind to lift your spirit.
> Turn, turn, turn
> With your feet upon the ground.

Fly, fly, fly
You are soaring and your senses
Take you upwards, take you outwards
And the world is spinning 'round.
Dance, dance, dance
It is time for celebration.
Turn, turn, turn,
See the happy couple there!
Fly, fly, fly
We'll go with them to the temple.
We'll be singing, we'll be dancing
There'll be music everywhere!

Women only

Well, well, well
So she's got herself a husband.
Soon, soon, soon
He'll be whispering in her ears.
And tonight, and tonight,
She might finally spend that treasure
She has guarded and protected,
She has hidden all these years!

Men only

Hey, hey, hey
Well tonight he'll be the hero
Standing tall,
Like a cedar, straight and proud.
And his bride,
Like the sweetest little flower
Growing up into his branches
She's the one who brings him down!

Repeat first verse, then only melody with dancing. Two circles, one of men, one of women; then they join into one surrounding the bride and groom.

Enter GILGAMESH as old man.

OLD GILGAMESH:
>It's mine. It's mine. I made it.
>It's for me. These halls, these doors, these stones
>All carry my name.
>My name... My name is...
>This is all for me... For me.
>The dancing is for me, and the wedding, to my honor.
>The bride is also for me.

1st CITIZEN:
>Go on, get away. This is no place for you.

2nd CITIZEN:
>Who is that?
>What does he want?
>Is he drunk or just feeble?

3rd CITIZEN:
>He's just a beggar.
>There seem to be more and more of them every day.

4th CITIZEN:
>It's time for the journey!
>Time to go to the temple! Enna awaits!
>The dwelling of Ishtar, the goddess of love!
>Come and join us!

The chorus resume song and dance. The bride and groom are held aloft and taken into the auditorium, the audience following.

OLD GILGAMESH:
>It is all for me.
>The music is mine, and the celebration.
>I've come back to my city – the city I built.
>The city that stands in my name...

My name… My name!
I have journeyed and labored.
I am worn out. I'm weary. I know secrets.
I know mysteries. I can tell you stories…
My father was Lugulbanda, a priest in this city.
My mother is Ninsun, a goddess. A goddess!
Immortal! But I'm not – immortal. I am mortal.
I'm old. I am dying.

By now all should have entered the auditorium. If not, OLD GILGAMESH
continues and/or repeats these mutterings until the ensemble is on stage and the
audience in their seats. The stage resembles the Temple of ISHTAR, the Goddess
and protector of Uruk.

FATHER OF THE BRIDE:
> My friends!
> A great welcome to you on this happy occasion.
> My daughter has married. Our youngest and dearest
> Will leave our safe home.
> She is too old now for keeping away from the world.
> She's grown up, and has chosen a new place for warmth,
> And for work, and for love, with her husband.
> And a finer young man no father,
> Or mother could hope for in Uruk.

Making offerings to the Temple of Ishtar, he prays.

> May their table be filled with the fruits of their labor.
> May their home always ring with the joy
> Of their children. May they remember the gods,
> And remember each other. And may their life
> Bring the pleasure that they cannot find alone.
> Enough talking!
> Now let music and dancing be the start of their journey,
> And happiness keep them together, all their days!

OLD GILGAMESH:

Wait! Just a minute! I demand your attention!

Music stops

FATHER:

What is it, old man?

If you wish us well, you are welcome to join us.

Who are you, and what is it that you want?

OLD GILGAMESH:

I have journeyed and labored. I've seen... many things!

Mountains, as high as the heavens;

And darkness, black as water, and endless.

Lions live in the mountains. I've killed them.

And giants, I've faced them too.

These walls, made of burnt brick and polished,

I built them! They are mine. This city is mine.

And these people. (He grows louder)

I'm Gilgamesh! King of Uruk!

I've returned to you!

I was blessed by the gods.

But they also cursed me.

They granted me kingship, but not immortality.

The citizens mock him.

FIRST CITIZEN:

You're Gilgamesh, the great King of Uruk,

The strongest city in Mesopotamia?

SECOND CITIZEN:

You're Gilgamesh, who slew the bull of heaven

In defiance of the great goddess Ishtar?

THIRD CITIZEN:

    You are Gilgamesh, who took every new bride on her wedding night –

    And any other woman he desired in Uruk?

    Oh, welcome, great king.

    We are ready to be commanded by your power!

All laugh.

VARIOUS CITIZENS:

    --Take him out!

    --Get him out!

    --He's upsetting the wedding.

    --We don't need to be reminded of Gilgamesh on this happy occasion.

The citizens gently push OLD GILGAMESH aside. He tries to resist, but cannot.

FOURTH CITIZEN (*Making offerings to Ishtar*):

    May the home of the bride and the bridegroom be peaceful!

    May your children bring joy to your household!

OLD GILGAMESH (*Addresses the Temple*):

    Ishtar, a curse on your city!

    May your children wither and die in their mothers' wombs,

    Rather than live in their parents' ignorance!

    May the people of Uruk, my people, be afflicted

    With madness and plague if they will not listen to my story.

    For it were madmen and fools who brought glory to Uruk,

    And the glory you seek is a plague

    Which blinds you to one another.

    I am Gilgamesh, fifth king of Uruk.

    I have journeyed and labored, am worn out and weary.

    I have seen the abyss, the secret and terror of life.

    Beyond the mountains of Mashu, at the end of the earth,

    Lives Utnapishtim, who survived the great flood.

    He told me the answer, he showed me the secret,

But… you don't believe me.
You only believe in me.
My city is not mine.
It belongs to a legend, to a fiction which no longer exists –
And perhaps never did.

Enter ISHTAR as an old woman. There is a slow build of drum rhythm through this speech as it flashbacks to the time when GILGAMESH reigned. Now we are witnessing a wedding that took place in the past. During ISHTAR's speech, the wedding attendees each take a character to enact the story. There is a tension built between the person who is to assume young Gilgamesh and the one who will play ENKIDU.

OLD WOMAN/ISHTAR:
Gilgamesh was young, he was beautiful.
No man could match him in strength or courage.
Uruk gleamed with the richness of lapis and gold.
The city was walled all around with thick stone work.
The outer wall shined with the brilliance of copper.
The inner wall was made of burnt brick, all polished.
In the whole world, there was no city like it.
The gods created Gilgamesh.
Two-thirds god and one-third man they made him.
Adad, the storm god, endowed him with courage.
Shamash, the god of the sun, made him radiant.
In beauty and strength no man was his equal.
He was proud, and his lust left no bride with her bridegroom.
No wife with her husband.
The people of Uruk were raised by his drum.
The lifeboat of the city was his command.

Drum crescendos to when young GILGAMESH enters. The wedding guests immediately form a barrier to the bride. GILGAMESH slowly inspects the wedding. The guests offer themselves for inspection, offer food, gifts, trying to distract or appease him as he moves towards the bride.

VARIOUS CITIZENS:

> --Let him pass. Don't stop him.
>
> --Keep him away from her.
>
> --Keep her silent!

FATHER OF THE BRIDE:

> You are most welcome to our celebration,
> Royal King Gilgamesh. We hope that our offerings
> May bring you pleasure.

GILGAMESH:

> I see many riches – fine oils, sweet perfumes,
> And succulent meats.
> It pleases me that my city can provide such delicacies –
> And my greatest pleasure is in the sampling
> Of first fruits.

He takes the bride by the hand.

GROOM:

> No! You shall not have her. She is mine!

He challenges GILGAMESH to the ritual wrestling match. This is done without words, but with formal recognized physical action. As OLD WOMAN/ISHTAR continues, GILGAMESH very deliberately breaks one of the GROOM's arms and leg, then forcefully picks up the bride by her hair, and carries her around the stage. This bride becomes a symbol of all brides in Uruk.

OLD WOMAN/ISHTAR:

> And so it continued, as Gilgamesh reigned.
> The city prospered, but his people had no voice.
> At the competitions he was often challenged,
> But never defeated, and his oppression turned to cruelty.
> Until one day here came a new challenger.

*Enter ENKIDU, shaped something between man and animal. He looks like a
stranger among the citizens.*

ENKIDU:

> I challenge you, Gilgamesh, with a bold voice.
> And I proclaim my strength equal to yours.
> GILGAMESH needn't respond verbally. They square off in the ritual
> fashion, as above. ENKIDU attacks first with a fierce, wild cry. He is
> not thrown. As ENKIDU and GILGAMESH wrestle the crowd
> gathers around them.

VARIOUS CITIZENS:

> --Who is he who challenges Gilgamesh?
> --Where is he from?
> --He is wild and untrained. Gilgamesh will destroy him.
> --He still stands! They are locked like wild bulls!
> --Was he sent by the gods? Who has seen him before?
> --Where does this challenger come from?

*GILGAMESH and ENKIDU wrestle for a few minutes, but neither can overcome
the other. Entangled and twisted in one another, they move about the stage. The
crowd moves with them. Eventually the crowd completely obscures them from
the view as the two moves offstage.*

END PROLOGUE

SCENE ONE

The Discovery of Enkidu to the battle with Gilgamesh

GILGAMESH's palace. STALKER enters, very agitated.

STALKER:

> I have seen him!
> At the watering place on the plain,
> A creature like no other: like a man,
> Yet not a man.
> A first day I have seen him, and a second and a third.
> Each day at the watering place.
> He ranges endlessly over the hills.
> Endlessly feeds on grass with the animals.
> He drinks the clear water with the gazelles.
> The wild beasts are his companions.
> But his eyes . . . His eyes fix on me like
> The light of a single star in a red sky.

GILGAMESH:

    Slowly, and calmly, now tell us.
    What does he look like,
    This wild man of the plains?

STALKER:

    All covered with hair,
    Like Sumuqan, the cattle god.
    The hair of his head is long, like a woman's.
    He is quick as an antelope, who he lives with like brothers.
    But his strength and his boldness surpass them.
    I have seen him take a wolf by the neck
    And crack its bones to protect the gazelles.
    Like a shooting star of Anu the sky god,
    His power is awesome.

GILGAMESH:

    If indeed he exists, he is some kind of demon,
    Created by the gods to inhabit the plains.
    Or perhaps some other kind of man.
    A true child of the earth, who shuns the cities
    And lives with the beasts in the wild.
    Beware of him, but do not fear him.
    Go about your work, lay your traps,
    Dig your pits, but always have your bow at the ready.

STALKER:

    But I can't go about my work?
    He tears out the traps I set,
    He fills the pits I dig.
    He allows the beasts to slip through my hands.
    In the wilderness he does not let me work.
    For terror I cannot go near him.
    For terror I will not return to the plains.

GILGAMESH:

>Then I shall gather a party of hunters,
>And I myself shall slay
>This half-man who makes you tremble.

NINSUN:

>Gilgamesh: if he is a creature
>Created and beloved by the gods,
>It is not wise to destroy him
>And bring him before us.

GILGAMESH exits. NINSUN addresses the STALKER.

NINSUN:

>In Uruk is the temple precinct, called Eanna.
>There the temple of Ishtar, the goddess of love
>Is tended by priestesses, skilled
>In the arts which no man may resist.
>Go to the temple. Take away with you a temple courtesan.
>Let her conquer this creature with a power equal to his own.

Exit NINSUN. Enter ISHTAR.

ISHTAR:

>A young hunter came to the temple of Ishtar
>A strange tale he told us,
>Of a free and wild man, not tamed by the city.
>We sent with the hunter a woman,
>A priestess skilled in the powers of order
>To wait for the man-beast at the place of clear water.
>When he comes to the watering place
>She will take off her clothes. She will show him
>Her strong beauty.
>When he sees her, he will come to her.
>His power will be subdued, and his animals will turn from him
>And shun him forever.

(The STALKER, the PRIESTESS along with three women are at the watering place. In the background we see GILGAMESH sleeping with his head on NINSUN's lap. MUSIC: "The Woman Speaks to Enkidu." She sings a lullaby to GILGAMESH.)

STALKER:

>We went on our journey, far out on the plains.
>For three days we traveled away from the city
>Until finally we came to the watering place.
>The pool was quiet.
>Only small birds came near it.
>We waited, but the man-beast did not appear.
>In the night, we could hear the wolves and lions
>As we shivered and waited underneath the dark sky.
>One day, a second day, we sat by the water.
>On the third dawn, the wild animals began to arrive.

1st WOMAN:

>They approached and their hearts grew light in the waters.
>Great beasts and small, all are nourished by Ea,
>The god of sweet waters.

STALKER:

>There he is! That's the man-beast!
>He seems one with the animals, but his eyes flash like lightning.
>Don't go near him; he could tear us to pieces!
>There! He sees us! Take your courage now and approach him.
>Show him your strong beauty, let him come close to you.
>Tame him with the wisdom of Ishtar.

(The PRIESTESS approaches the water, ENKIDU and the animals are on the other side. They shy away, but he is fascinated. In the background, a subtle rhythm and/or solo recorder is heard. She approaches the pool slowly, removes her clothes, and begins to wash herself, beginning with her hair. She begins to sing. Her voice mixes with NINSUN's lullaby to create a soothing melody. It is

her voice that seduces him. A chorus of the STALKER and three maids narrates the following.)

1st WOMAN:

> And the people had cried to the gods for salvation
> From Gilgamesh, king and tyrant of Uruk.
> "Is this the shepherd of Uruk," they wondered,
> Who takes girls from their mothers
> And brides from their bridegrooms?"

STALKER:

> The voice of the priestess filled his ears
> With sweet rhythms,
> All day and he first night he waited and listened.

2nd WOMAN:

> The gods heard the lament of the people of Uruk.
> They called on Anu, the father of the gods.
> "It was you who brought Gilgamesh into the city.
> And now his oppression brings sadness and pain."

STALKER:

> Enkidu drew closer, and the woman remained.
> The breeze carried her scent to him,
> And his senses were racing.

3rd WOMAN:

> Anu called to Aruru, the Great Mother Goddess"
> "You created humanity, work you powers now again.
> Make a second for Gilgamesh, an image equal to him.
> Let them fight one another and bring peace to the city."

STALKER:

> He approached, raised his arm to her,
> And brought it down gently

As her hair, shoulder, and breast
Melted the strength of his hand.

1ST WOMAN:

And the goddess Aruru pinched clay from the river
And she formed it, and smoothed it, placed it deep in the wilderness.
In the darkness and silence she gave life to Enkidu.
He grew strong in the forest and his heart knew no fear.

STALKER:

The priestess drew his face to hers
And her lips touched his mouth.
She drew his breath from him, gave her own in return,
And Enkidu felt a life he had not known before.

2nd WOMAN:

His whole body covered with hair, rich and beautiful.
His locks grew like the grain of the gods of the field.
Two-thirds beast and one-third man Aruru had made him.
He was quick and strong, but alone on the plain.

STALKER:

Enkidu gazed up at the priestess before him.
In her eyes he could see her spirit, and his own.
His heart cried out in both anguish and ecstasy
But its language was one he did not understand.

3rd WOMAN:

He knew neither people nor homeland, this wild man.
He fed and drank with the antelopes, free on the plain.
No man was his equal in strength or in cunning.
Like Gilgamesh, he longed for a partner and friend.

STALKER:

On the sixth night she opened herself to Enkidu.
Scent and vision, heart, and breath he had not known before.

She embraced him, engulfed him,
And the light of the stars blazed in glory
As the night sky slowly faded to dawn.

1st WOMAN:

On the seventh day they both rested.
Man and woman, beast and goddess lay upon the cool sands.

STALKER:

Enkidu tries to rise up, but his body prevents him.
His knees will not move, and his legs have grown weak.
The animals – panthers, antelope, gazelles, wild dogs and wolves
All turn from him; they no longer know him.
He tries to follow, but it is as predicted:
He has no more strength. The animals shun him.
He both feels this, and knows it, for his mind has been opened.

PRIESTESS:

Enkidu. Enkidu, that is what men will call you.
Son of Ea, who gives wisdom,
And Aruru, the Great Goddess.
You have become wise like a god, Enkidu,
You have gained knowledge and vision.
Why do you wish to still live in the wilderness?
I will teach you the ways of men – and you will conquer them.
You will learn to eat bread, and drink strong wine,
And I will lead you to Eanna, the precinct of Ishtar,
In the city where Gilgamesh holds all power.
And I will show you this Gilgamesh, who stands
Like a wild bull over all the people.
Shamash the sun god protects him
And Anu, and Enlil, and Eahave opened his mind.
You will challenge him with your boldness
And Uruk will be at peace.

STALKER:

He heard her words and listened to what she said.

The wisdom of the woman found his heart.

He formed his mouth, and Enkidu spoke:

ENKIDU:

Come with me, where Gilgamesh is.

Like a wild bull, where he stands above his people.

I will shout to him, I will shout in Uruk:

"I am powerful. I am Enkidu.

The strength of the plains and the beasts is in me."

PRIESTESS:

Even before you have come out of the mountains

Gilgamesh will have seen you in his dreams.

STALKER:

She took a part of her clothing and covered him.

Another part she kept for herself.

She took his hand and led him like a child to the sheepfold.

The shepherds clustered around him…

Exit ENKIDU, The STALKER, the priestess and the women. The animals follow in a different direction. GILGAMESH jolts awake as if from a nightmare.

GILGAMESH:

Mother!!

Mother, divine goddess, I have had a dream

Which has made me afraid.

There was a star in the heavens,

A great and blazing light.

Like a shooting start of Anu if fell upon me.

I tried to lift it; it was too much for me.

I tired to move it; it would not budge.

The people of Uruk swarmed around it.

The men kissed it, the woman praised it,
Until I myself embraced it with love,
And you compared it as an equal to me.

NINSUN:

My son, noble Gilgamesh, be not afraid.
This star is your companion, sent from heaven to comfort you.
Like a shooting star it falls upon you.
You try to lift it; it is too much for you.
You try to move it; you are not able.
To me, this star is your equal.
And like a brother, you embrace it.

GILGAMESH:

And I had a second dream:
In the midst of Uruk a great axe fell.
It was magnificent, with a great stone blade
And a shaft of cedar.
The people of Uruk swarmed around it, amazed.
I embraced, raised it up, and lay it at your feet,
So that you compared it with me.

NINSUN:

The meaning of your dream is this:
The star, the axe, are you powerful companion.
His strength is great; he will save his friend from danger.
Like a shooting star on Anu his strength is awesome.
You embraced the star and the axe, and I
Compared them to you as equals.
This star, this axe will be your brother.
Two-thirds beast, one-third man he was made by the gods.
You yourself are two-thirds divine, one-third mortal.
Together you bring into balance the forces of life.
You will have many victories, he will bring you great happiness,

But he will also be taken from you, torn away from your side,
And your grief will take you to worlds yet unknown.

GILGAMESH:

But where will I find him? When will I see him?

NINSUN:

That is all Gilgamesh. When you see him
You shall embrace him. Go now and sleep.

*The focus is on STALKER, ENKIDU, and PRIESTESS, who teaches ENKIDU the
ways of humans. ENKIDU mimes the actions described by the STALKER.*

STALKER:

Enkidu was used to eating the grass from the plains.
He would suck the milk from wild animals for strength.
When the shepherds set down bread for him, he just stared at it.
No one had taught him about how men eat food.
He took it but it did not please him.
The shepherds offered him strong wine,
Which he had never drunk before.
It was the woman who taught him the ways of men.

PRIESTESS:

Take he bread, Enkidu, as life requires.
It is from the fruit of the grasses of the plains,
Molded and formed by men.
Drink the wine. It is a gift of the gods
Sent to make men's life more pleasant.
Drink, as is the custom of the land.

STALKER:

So Enkidu ate the bread, and drank the wine,
Seven goblets.
And Enkidu learned the customs of men.

1st WOMAN:

> Enkidu wore clothes; he pulled back his hair,
> And his face became radiant.
> He took up a weapon and protected the sheep.
> He caught wolves, captured lions, and became
> The guardian of the sheepfold.
> Now the shepherds could lie down at night
> With Enkidu to watch then; a hero like no other.

ENKIDU:

> Tell me of Uruk and of Gilgamesh, its protector.
> What is the city like? And what do the people do there?

PRIESTESS:

> In Uruk, every day there is a festival
> With strings and drums, there is music and dancing,
> And everyone drinks wine.
> The people are resplendent, with wide belts and bright clothes,
> And the city is filled with riches and beauty.
> In the temple of Ishtar, the holy priestesses preserve
> The arts of life and of pleasure.
> They are filled with the joy of their sex, with life-joy,
> And their energy radiates throughout the city.

ENKIDU:

> And Gilgamesh? Did he create all this?
> Through what power had he been blessed
> With such a kingdom?

PRIESTESS:

> The gods created Gilgamesh;
> Two-thirds god and one-third man they made him.
> His mother in Ninsun, a goddess of Uruk.
> His father, a high priest in Uruk – a mortal.
> Shamash, the god of the sun, made him radiant.

Adad, the storm god, endowed him with courage.
I will show you this hero, whom they call the joy-woe man.
He is beautiful in his manhood, tall and straight as a cedar.
He is stronger than you – always active, never resting.
In the city of Uruk he built temples to Anu,
The god of the sky, and to Ishtar,
The goddess of love – and destruction.
And the walls, how they gleam, surrounding the city.
The walls are his masterwork.
The outer wall shines with the brilliance of copper,
The towers, black porphyry from the pillage of Babylon.
The inner wall is made of burnt brick, each one flawless,
Crafted with the blood of the people of Uruk.

ENKIDU:

What do you mean, "crafted in blood"?
Does he not protect his people?

PRIESTESS:

He brings glory to Uruk – and terror.
He is proud, and his lust leaves no bride with her bridegroom,
No wife with her husband. The young men are taken
To battle his enemies. The people of Uruk
Are raised by his drum and taken as laborers.
Year after year building walls in his name.
The lifeblood of Uruk is his to command.
He brought riches and glory, but also oppression.
And sometimes, the people cry out to the gods,
"Is this a king, strong, shining, and thoughtful?
The shepherd who cares for his people?"

ENKIDU:

And the gods do not answer?

2nd WOMAN:

    It was the gods who gave him the city in the first place!

    The temples of Anu and Ishtar fill

    One-third of the city. As long as they profit,

    The people mean nothing!

ENKIDU:

    But a king may be challenged. Are there no young men

    Who can defeat him at the games?

    Is there no wrestler to take down his arrogance and pride?

STALKER:

    Many have tried, but his strength is too great.

    I myself faced him once, and I'll tell you this much:

    I'd rather meet six lions in the mountain pass

    Than try my luck against Gilgamesh again.

3rd WOMAN:

    It's an outrage, the way he lords it over his people.

    My own mother has told me of her wedding night.

    He lets the drums sound, the banns of marriage,

    Announcing the union of a man and his wife,

    But he goes first! The husband comes after.

    This "King" of Uruk defiles sacred customs

    And brings shame to the people he's supposed to protect.

ENKIDU:

    It is time. Take me to him.

    Let me see this great city

    And the wild bull who calls himself a king.

    I will challenge him with a loud voice.

    I will cry out in Uruk: "I am powerful!

    The strength of the plains and the beasts is in me!

    I am Enkidu."

OLD GILGAMESH:

> I remember: as he entered he city, the woman walked in front.
> With Enkidu behind her.
> They walked through the market place,
> On the way to the bride's house.
> This strange wild creature, more beast than man,
> Being led through the city by a woman ...
> But the people swarmed around him saying,
> "Who is he who challenges Gilgamesh?"

Fade back to citizens watching ENKIDU enter the city. MUSIC: "A Hero Has Come."

1st CITIZEN:

> Where is he from?

2nd CITIZEN:

> He is like Gilgamesh in build, only shorter.

3rd CITIZEN:

> He is stronger than Gilgamesh. A challenger has come!

1st CITIZEN:

> A hero has arrived to stand up to Gilgamesh.
> For Gilgamesh the godlike, an equal is here!

The ensemble forms image from end of wedding, GILGAMESH carrying bride.

ENKIDU:

> I challenge you, Gilgamesh, with a bold voice,
> And I proclaim my strength equal to yours.

GILGAMESH:

> Who comes here? Who dares

To challenge my power?
Who are you, whose bold voice exceeds his small reason?

ENKIDU:

A child of the plains, brother to the gazelles,
Part man, and part beast the gods have created me,
And my strength is the strength of a lion in rage.

GILGAMESH:

Part man, and part god, I have founded this city.
My kingship is known to all people on earth.
Still you stand here before me, bold and reckless with pride?

ENKIDU:

I challenge you, Gilgamesh. I will not leave Uruk
Until I have tested your power against me.

OLD GILGAMESH:

He blocked the way with his foot.
He would not let me pass.
I regarded this new challenger as I would any other:
A nuisance, a pastime – but there was something about him.
In his eyes, a light, like a shooting star …
And the people were shouting,
"An equal for Gilgamesh has arrived."
We seized one another at the bride house gate.
We wrested, locked together like wild bulls.
The doorposts shattered, and the walls of the bride-house shook.
We fought in the streets, through the entire city quarter.
Neither one could throw the other.
All day long we fought, in the dust of the streets
Until finally, before the temple of Ishtar
I planted my foot, bent my knee,
Seized Enkidu with a powerful grip and threw him to the ground.
But my anger subsided, I turned slowly away.

Enkidu rose and faced me, but his arms were weak.
His strength had left him.

GILGAMESH:

You were born in the wilderness.
Like a shooting star from heaven you fell upon me.
Your strength is great.

OLD GILGAMESH:

Enkidu lifted his arms; eyes filled with tears.
He formed his mouth, and spoke slowly to me.

ENKIDU:

Friend.

They embrace. The people of Uruk rejoice, and fall into celebration of the partnership of GILGAMESH and ENKIDU.

END SCENE ONE

SCENE TWO

Preparation for the Forest Journey

GILGAMESH and ENKIDU in the palace.

GILGAMESH:

> Before you arrived, my heart was restless.
> My city had wealth and riches,
> My people are strong and fear no enemies,
> But I had no companion, no equal.
> You can become the axe at my side,
> Together we are greater than any one hero.
> But this city is no place for us.

ENKIDU:

> The city offers many pleasures and comforts,
> Which the beasts of the plains do not enjoy.
> But a freedom is lost here, and a sense of life.
> Still, I do not think that you are ready
> To abandon your city for a life on the plains.

GILGAMESH:

 Not abandon the city but bring greater glory to it.

 We will not roam the plains; we will conquer the forest.

 The dark forest of cedar that lies far to the north.

ENKIDU:

 I would not advise it, Gilgamesh.

 I have been to the forest, I have seen its darkness.

 The forest runs for 10,000 leagues, and lets in no sunlight.

 Its cedars are rich, their wood everlasting,

 But the trees are sacred, and protected by the gods.

 It is said that Ishtar has a temple there,

 All made of fragrant wood,

 In the midst of the cedar.

GILGAMESH:

 And so should we have one! A great house of cedar!

 It is the richest wood in all the world.

 Its strength is unsurpassed, its beauty renowned

 And its fragrance pleases even the gods.

 Why should we not have it? To Uruk I have brought

 An abundance of gold, lapis lazuli, and copper.

 Great stones and burnt brick surround the city,

 And our wealth surpasses all cities of the world.

 But cedar I do not have.

 If we conquer the forest, our glory will last forever.

ENKIDU:

 But perhaps you have not heard, friend,

 Of the guardian of that great forest.

 A giant dwells there: he is called Humbaba.

 To guard the cedar forest and to terrify mankind

 Enlil has appointed him.

 His voice is like a storm-flood

 His breath like fire

And his jaws like death itself.
He can unleash the seven terrors which the gods have given him.
I tell you, it would be no equal match if we challenged Humbaba.

GILGAMESH:
But the forest is huge, as you said,
It extends 10,000 leagues in every direction.
We will go in and fell the cedars
With great axes made by the craftsmen of Uruk.
No man has conquered the forest,
But you and I are not ordinary men.
With the cedarwood we will build a temple in Uruk
More glorious than any ever seen.
My city shall be known throughout the world
As the richest and most powerful ever!

ENKIDU:
Humbaba has a thousand eyes
And the watchman of the forest never sleeps.
If a fawn should stir, even 60 leagues distant
He hears her.
And the watchman has watchmen who guard every tree.

GILGAMESH:
Oh, where is the man who can climb up to heaven!
Only the gods live forever, Enkidu!
As for us, our days are numbered,
Our occupations are like a breath of wind.
How is it that you are already afraid –
You who have the strength and courage of a lion.
I will go first, even though I am your lord,
And you may safely stay behind, calling to me:
"Go forward, there is nothing to fear!"

ENKIDU:

>But why do you need to do this?
>Humbaba is evil, but he does not threaten your people.
>The cedar is precious, but your riches abound.
>No man has conquered Humbaba, and you already command
>Great respect among men and even the gods.
>You have no need of riches or power.
>Why must you embark on this dangerous journey?

GILGAMESH:

>My name is not yet written with the names of the famous.
>I am powerful, but I have not yet fulfilled my destiny.
>I have looked over the wall, and I see the bodies floating in the river.
>Men live, and die, and are forgotten
>And that will be my fate as well.
>Here in the city, man dies with despair in his heart.
>For that reason, I will go to the land of the cedar.
>I will set up my name where the names of the famous are written,
>And where no man's name is written, I will raise a monument.
>Even if I die, I will leave behind a name that endures.
>They will say, "Gilgamesh has fallen in battle with ferocious
>Humbaba."
>Through generations of my house, they will say it, and remember me.

ENKIDU:

>If it must be, I will not leave you.
>I will lead the way, for I know where the forest is.
>And I will stand beside you in the face of Humbaba.

GILGAMESH:

>We will order weapons made: great axes of nine score pounds,
>With which we will cut the cedar.
>And great swords with heavy blades
>And pommels and hilts of the finest metals and stones
>A bow with arrows to pierce the heart of Humbaba,

And armor to protect ourselves from his terrors.
Come, let us go to Ninsun, the great queen goddess,
My mother. She will give us her blessing,
And lay out a wise path for us.
She will pray for us to Shamash for protection.
They approach NINSUN, who is accompanied by maids.

GILGAMESH:

Ninsun, great goddess and wise
Who bore me and who knows my heart,
I long to set out on a journey,
Far off to the cedar forest, to the place of Humbaba.
I must travel a road I cannot know.
I will face a battle which I know nothing about.
For Humbaba is fierce, and possesses seven terrors.
From the day I go until the day I return,
Until I have destroyed Humbaba and conquered the cedar forest,
I ask you to pray for me to Shamash,
God of the sun and the light, for protection.

NINSUN:

Gilgamesh, you are a great king and powerful ruler.
You are blessed by the gods with strength, beauty, and wisdom.
And you are my son. Now listen to me:
Do not go on this journey.
The cedar is a sacred precinct of Ishtar,
And her servant Humbaba guards it well.
It is not meant for you; you do not require it.
I tell you, this adventure can only bring you sadness.

GILGAMESH:

But Humbaba is evil! He is an evil that Shamash abhors.
It is I who will destroy that evil,
And Shamash will protect me,
My name will be known among the gods.

NINSUN:

>Enkidu, you are not a child of my body,
>
>But I have seen you in dreams.
>
>You are strong, you are brave, and a good companion for my son.
>
>Here, before the votresses of my order,
>
>I adopt you as my own.
>
>Serve me as you would serve the parents you do not have.
>
>And serve Gilgamesh as your brother.
>
>I entrust my son to you; bring him back safely.

GILGAMESH and ENKIDU leave the temple.

>Shamash, why have you given my son
>
>This restless heart? Why did you give it to him?
>
>You push him now to go on a long journey,
>
>To battle Humbaba.
>
>It is a road he does not know.
>
>It is a battle he cannot understand.
>
>It is a task which will bring him sadness and pain.

OLD GILGAMESH (As GILGAMESH and ENKIDU prepare to leave for the forest):

>We had the weapons brought: great axes and swords
>
>Which we kept by our sides. We announced to the city
>
>Our plan to defeat Humbaba, and conquer the cedar.
>
>The young ones cheered us on.
>
>And the old ones were full of advice:

A YOUNG CITIZEN:

>"Good luck, Gilgamesh!
>
>May you return safely and bring glory to the city of Uruk!"

1st OLD CITIZEN:

>"Don't trust your own strength, Gilgamesh. Keep a clear eye!"

2nd OLD CITIZEN:

> You are young, Gilgamesh; your courage pushed you too far.
> You cannot know what this enterprise means.

3nd OLD CITIZEN:

> Humbaba is not like men who die.
> His weapons are such that none stands against them.
> His breath is like the torrent of the storm,
> And his jaws like death itself.

4th OLD CITIZEN:

> Against Humbaba it is no equal struggle.
> Gilgamesh, consider well what you do.

GILGAMESH:

> How shall I answer them, these wise counselors?
> Shall I say that I'll sit here the rest of my life?
> I am going to see this great creature who men say is so terrible.
> I will conquer the cedar wood, and defeat this great evil.
> I will show him the strength of the city of Uruk
> To this enterprise I am committed,
> And my name will be remembered.

2nd OLD CITIZEN:

> Let Enkidu go first! He knows the way and has been to the forest.
> The one who goes in front guards his companion!

1st OLD CITIZEN:

> Beware of the passes as you go through the mountains.
> Keep a keen eye out for dangers ahead!

3rd OLD CITIZEN:

> Remember your guardian god, Lugulbanda.
> Make offerings to him, that he'll stand beside you!

4th OLD CITIZEN:

>Every night dig a well,
>
>Offer clear water to Shamash,
>
>And in the morning wash your feet as you welcome the dawn!

ENKIDU:

>Enough! Forward! We will not be afraid!
>
>Follow me; I know where he lives,
>
>And the path that he walks.
>
>Let the counselors go back; now no more delays!

YOUNG CITIZEN:

>Go, Gilgamesh. May your god bring you back to the houses of Uruk.

NINSUN:

>I pray to you, Shamash, and to your bride Aia, the dawn:
>
>From the day he goes until the day he returns,
>
>Until he returns from the land of the cedars,
>
>Protect King Gilgamesh and guide his path.
>
>I pray to you, Shamash, and to your bride Aia,
>
>You who give light and strength to the earth:
>
>Guide your servants, Enkidu and Gilgamesh,
>
>Whom you have made restless
>
>And who long for glory.
>
>I pray to you, Shamash, and to your bride Aia,
>
>They travel a road they do not know.
>
>They face a battle they cannot understand.
>
>From the day they go until the day they return
>
>Guide their steps safely back to their homeland.

NINSUN along with People of Uruk continue to pray as the Scene fades to black.

END SCENE TWO

SCENE THREE

The Forest Journey

OLD GILGAMESH:

      We traveled across the plains, like two young heroes.

      We traveled 20 leagues, then had something to eat.

      Another 30 leagues and we stopped for the night.

      We traveled for 3 days, and in 3 days we walked

      As far as a journey of a month and 2 weeks.

      From the top of the seventh mountain we could see the cedar forest.

ENKIDU:

      I will go first, down into the forest.

      I know the sounds of the animals, and the colors of the trees.

      If the way is safe, I will tell you to follow me.

GILGAMESH:

      Shall we not go together, to challenge Humbaba?

      Together, you and I, who can defeat us?

ENKIDU:

> Humbaba is not like man, to be challenged directly.
> We must first find a way into the forest, and catch him unaware.

He goes down to the forest.

GILGAMESH (*Alone*):

> These mountains are strange to me; their sound and their light
> Have a language. The wind whispers
> To the sky, and the clouds seem to answer in conspiracy against me.
> I have lived too long in the city, where my word creates order.
> I see ghosts in the shadows, and spirits in the stones.

ENKIDU (*running back*):

> Aaaahhh! Gilgamesh!
> Do not go down to the forest. I tell you
> The danger is great. I found a gate, but when I opened it,
> My hand lost all its strength. We should not enter there
> We should return to the city.

GILGAMESH:

> What? Have we come all this way for nothing?
> Don't talk like a coward.
> You, who were raised with beasts,
> You're afraid of the forest?
> Come stand by me;
> Together we'll enter the land of cedar.
> Fear nothing; forget death, and your weakness shall pass.
> If we fall, we leave an enduring name behind us.
> This gate cannot keep us from entering the forest
> Where the riches of cedar await.

They enter.

ENKIDU:

> The trees are like nothing I have seen with my eyes!
> Tall and dense, like a cool green temple.
> Like a shaded sanctuary.

GILGAMESH:

> And there, far ahead, is the mountain of cedars
> Where Ishtar has established her throne.
> There is a path cut through the forest;
> Broad and green;
> Leading to the heart of the mountain.
> We will follow it, until we meet Humbaba.

OLD GILGAMESH:

> Again, we traveled 20 leagues and had something to eat.
> Another 30, and we stopped for the night.
> All day we neither saw nor heard Humbaba.
> I dug a well before the setting sun,
> Made an offering to Shamash.
> And in the morning washed my feet.
> To welcome the dawn.

GILGAMESH:

> Shamash, who dwells beyond the mountains,
> Remember us tonight in this darkness, in the forest.
> Tomorrow we face Humbaba;
> We fight him for your glory,
> And to make ourselves a name.
> Give us a favorable dream on this night,
> So that we might meet Aia, the dawn, with strong hearts
> And face the task we have undertaken.
> Come Enkidu – let's lie down together,
> And protect one another from the cold of the mountain.
> Soon the night will pour down sleep upon us,
> And if Shamash sends us favorable dreams,
> It is a good omen.

They lie down. Spirits hover about them. It is cold and dark. The spirits make GILGAMESH's sleep uneasy. He wakes.

GILGAMESH:

What?! Did you call me? Did you wake me up?
I have had a dream, a terrible dream.
I seized hold of a wild bull in the wilderness.
It bellowed and stamped, and raised up the dust
Until the air was thick and the whole sky was dark.
My arms were paralyzed, I fell down on one knee.
And just as the bull was about to attack me,
Someone – I could not see who it was –
Gave me fresh water from his waterskin,
And the bull disappeared.

ENKIDU:

Friend, this dream is not terrible at all!
The wild bull you saw is Shamash the Protector.
When we need him, in our moment of greatest danger,
He will take our hands and give us strength.
As for the water-giver, that is your own guardian god, Lugulbanda,
Who cares for your good name.
With these gods to help us, together we will accomplish our task
And gain a fame which will never die.

They sleep. Spirits, as before. GILGAMESH awakens.

GILGAMESH:

What?! Who is there? Who wakes me? Enkidu?
My sleep is broken. I have dreamed again.
This time we were together, you and I,
In the deep gorge of a mountain.
The mountain was huge, and we were like flies beside it.
And suddenly, it fell, came crashing down
All around us.

My feet fell away from under me, and I was falling into the abyss.
But then, a blazing light shone out,
Brighter than the sun, and in it, a woman
Whose beauty surpassed anything seen on earth.
She pulled us out from under the mountain;
Gave us sweet water to drink,
And set our feet on firm ground.

ENKIDU:

Do not fear this dream! Tomorrow we will surely win!
The blazing light is Aia, the dawn; the mountain is Humbaba.
Tomorrow he will fall into the plain
In great chaos and confusion.
We shall seize him, and kill him
And our names will be raised up.

They sleep again. This time the spirits of the forest torment ENKIDU, more violently. He has an ominous dream of his own sickness and death. He wakes up, sees GILGAMESH sleeping, but does not wake him. He is visibly shaken. Just as he lies down again to rest, GILGAMESH wakes up.

GILGAMESH:
Did you call me? Did you wake me?

Why am I terrified, and my arms and legs numb?
Friend, I had a third dream, this one worse than the others.
The heavens roared and the earth billowed back.
The light of day disappeared; darkness fell over everything.
But in the darkness, lights flashed and fires blazed
And black clouds rained down death.
What does it mean, Enkidu? How can this be a good sign?

ENKIDU:

It is almost dawn. Let's go down from the mountain
And continue further along out way.

As GILGAMESH and ENKIDU journey through the forest, Sporadic voices are heard under their speeches.

VOICES:

> Who comes? Who comes? The forest is dark.
> Who comes? Who comes? His fortune is death.

GILGAMESH:

> Where is this Humbaba, this terror of the forest?
> We've wandered his paths for two days
> But he will not show his face.
> I don't believe he exists.

ENKIDU:

> Believe me, he is watching.
> His eye observes every quiver of the cedars.
> He hears even the smallest creature stirring.
> And the forest is filled with his servants.

VOICES:

> The cedar is sacred, the home of the gods.
> The watchman never sleeps.
> Who comes? Who comes? The forest is dark.
> Who comes? Who comes? His fortune is death.

GILGAMESH:

> Well, we won't wait for him to destroy us
> Before we have a chance to fight.
> We've come for the cedar, and the cedar shall be ours.

He takes up his axe.

> For the glory of Uruk, and the name of Gilgamesh,
> I strike down this cedarwood
> And claim it as my prize!

He cuts a tree. Thundering voice of HUMBABA is heard.

HUMBABA:

Who dares? Who dares the cedar to strike?
Who dares? Who dares the cedar to kill?

Gilgamesh strikes again.

Who comes? What man has courage to enter?
Who comes? What fool defies the dark cedar wood?

Gilgamesh strikes a third time. HUMBABA is louder

Who is this who has violated my forest?
I'll tear his limbs and make him food for the ravens!
I am Humbaba, guardian of the forest of Ishtar!

GILGAMESH and ENKIDU are gripped by fear. GILGAMESH tries to strike again, but is paralyzed. He falls down, unconscious.

ENKIDU:

Gilgamesh! Gilgamesh!
Lord of Kullab, King of Uruk!
What is this sleep that has overcome you?
The world grows dark, the forest is trembling!
Oh, Gilgamesh, how long will you lie like this?
Why has Shamash abandoned us?

As HUMBABA throws down a cedar to impale GILGAMESH, he wakes up and darts out of the way.

GILGAMESH:

I will not let my mother, Ninsun,
Mourn me in the city square.
Until we have fought this man, if man he is,
This god, if god he is, I will not return to the city!

ENKIDU:

> Friend, now we have see this monster
> And the terror he possesses!
> His teeth, long fangs, protrude from a mouth
> Which is twisted and foaming, searching for blood.
> His breath is like a storm-flood,
> And with one look of his eyes, he crushes the trees
> Of his own forest.
> If we don't turn back now
> We shall never see our city again!

GILGAMESH:

> Today is not the day that I'll go down to the underworld!
> Come, give me your help, and you shall have mine.
> Against the two of us, even this beast has no match.
> Now throw your fear away, and take up your axe.
> He who leaves the battle unfinished is never at peace.

HUMBABA attacks again.

ENKIDU:

> There he is! Now remember your boasts!
> He has put on one of the terrors, but not yet all seven.
> Quickly! Close in now, before he is armed!

GILGAMESH:

> Oh, Shamash, you have sent us into this battle,
> How are we to escape without your help now?
> Send the winds to our aid, to slow down this monster.
> The north wind, the whirlwind, the storm and the ice wind,
> The hot winds of the west, with their burning sand.
> Send these al to contain this beast!

ENKIDU:

> It's working! The strong winds blow around him

And close up his eyes.
He cannot move forward or back – now we have him!

GILGAMESH:

By the life of my mother and the glory of Shamash
I have entered your forest and will conquer your temple.
The cedar is mine!

HUMBABA:

Gilgamesh! Let me speak!
I have no mother, nor no god to protect me.
I was born of the mountain, and Enlil the sky god
Made me keeper of the forest.
Let me go free and the cedar is yours.
I will cut the trees for you,
I will build you a great palace.
I will be your servant all the days of my life.
Gilgamesh, I am not the evil you imagine.

GILGAMESH:

Perhaps he is right.
Like a snared bird, we have him.
As our servant, he can give us glory and fame
Beyond what we imagined.

ENKIDU:

Do not listen to him! You do not know his power!
He'll destroy the pathways of the forest
And trap us like mice.
The strongest of men is nothing
If his judgment is weak.

HUMBABA:

I can give you riches, Gilgamesh.
Fragrant cedarwood, enough to build cities!

Its value and beauty surpass even gold.
And your name shall be known throughout the world
As a king wise, wealthy, and powerful.

ENKIDU:

Do not hesitate, Gilgamesh!
Strike him now, or we're lost!
The winds will not hold him forever,
And once he is free, he'll unleash all his terrors.
Take up your axe and sword and strike
And I'll follow!

OLD GILGAMESH:

I trusted the words of Enkidu, my friend.
I took up the great sword and struck a blow
To the neck of Humbaba.
He cried out; Enkidu followed
With a second, a great gash to the chest.
With the third blow Humbaba fell at out feet.
In the forest, there followed confusion and chaos.
For the guardian of the cedar lay motionless on the ground.
For as far as two hundred leagues, the cedars shivered and quaked.
The mountains sighed, and the hills seemed to tremble
And at once the whole forest
For 10,000 leagues in every direction
Fell silent.
We cleansed ourselves, and offered incense to the gods.
We cut off the head and, under protection of Shamash,
Made our way back to Uruk.

END SCENE THREE

SCENE FOUR

The Bull of Heaven

In front of the temple of ISHTAR, in the city of Uruk. some citizens worship ISHTAR while others go about the business of the city. In one area young men challenge one another to wrestling matched, much more crudely than the matches in the first scene. After a while in the midst of one match, GILGAMESH and ENKIDU enter. The wrestling stops. All citizens stop what they are doing and in amazement stare at the two heroes who are carrying the head of HUMBABA. MUSIC: "Rejoicing Over Gilgamesh and Enkidu's Triumph Over Humbaba."

ISHTAR:

      The people of Uruk, relieved of oppression,

      Turned their love and devotion to their goddess Ishtar.

      No man had ever returned from the forest,

      For its guardian, Humbaba, was both quick and terrible.

      For many seasons the city was peaceful,

      And Ishtar provided for her worshipers.

But the people were fickle and remained unsatisfied.
They still longed for the glory of their former king.

GILGAMESH:

We have returned with the head of Humbaba!

ENKIDU:

The glory of cedar is ours!

VARIOUS CITIZENS:

-He has returned!
-King Gilgamesh had returned!
-With Enkidu, they have returned from the forest
with the head of Humbaba!
-The glory is theirs!
-The cedar is ours!
-All glory and power to Uruk!
-And to us!

1st CITIZEN:

Long live the names of Enkidu and Gilgamesh!

ALL:

Long live the names of Enkidu and Gilgamesh!

They fall into a chant of "GILGAMESH, hero, and king!" Repeat until interrupted by ISHTAR.

ISHTAR:

Welcome, Gilgamesh – hero and king of Uruk.
You have entered the forest, from which no man has returned.
You have slain the giant Humbaba, its guardian and keeper.
Your name shall surely be written with the names of heroes,
And the glory of Uruk shall be throughout time.
Your glory – and mine.

A king, and a goddess.

Our power and beauty shall know no equal.

Note: If music is used in this scene, it is possible that not all of this text would be used. MUSIC: "Song of Ishtar's Seduction and Gilgamesh's Rejection."

Come to me, Gilgamesh
Lie with me, Gilgamesh
Fragrance and pleasure and riches are yours.
Come to me, Gilgamesh
I'll make you my bridegroom
Your chariot shall be fashioned of lapis and gold
Its wheels shining copper, its horns precious amber.
Your horses shall be like the demons of wind.
Kings, rulers, and princes shall bow down before you.
Come, Gilgamesh, be my lover!

GILGAMESH:

Proud Ishtar, your offer astounds me.
I am not worthy of the love of a goddess.
What would I give you if I should take you as a wife?
Fine breads and rare meats, for you are already accustomed
To the food of the gods?
New garments and jewelry? You are already as radiant as the sun.
Oils for your body? I would tremble to offer it.
No, the gap between us is too wide, if I take you in marriage.

ISHTAR:

Enter this house – our house –
In the sweet scent of cedarwood.
Lie with me under cool palms, with sweet fragrance.
The glory of Uruk is yours – and mine.

GILGAMESH:

No! Keep away! Your love is a treachery!
Which of your lovers has loved you forever?
Which of your shepherds continues to please you?
Come, let me name them:
Tammuz, your first love, dwells now in the underworlds.
Year after year his wailing is heard
And your treatment of him is legend.

104

You once loved a shepherd, a young boy, and handsome.
He brought you cakes,
And slaughtered the best of his flock at your honor.
Now he's a wolf and his own dogs attack him.
And Ishullanu, the gardener, who brought you baskets of dates.
Every day he made your table rich with his fruits.
You struck him, and made him a reptile who dwells in the earth.
Like this would you love me, and share my glory?
Tell me, proud Ishtar, which of your lovers still lives?

ISHTAR:

Those lovers were mere men, not worthy of my glory.
They pleased me for a time, but their pride made them small.
You, Gilgamesh, are a true hero;
You are the flesh of the gods.
To you I can offer my love without shame.

GILGAMESH:

No – we will make you an offering of the fruits of our enterprise:
The head of Humbaba is yours!

GILGAMESH throws the head of HUMBABA at ISHTAR's foot, and walks away
with ENKIDU at his side. The citizens are divided in their loyalties. MUSIC:
"Ishtar's Revenge."

ISHTAR (to herself):

Insults? And mockery? Oh, Gilgamesh, "hero,"
Your pride is your misery. Death your reward.
Anu! My father! This man has insulted me!
Ishtar, protector of Uruk, and goddess
Of love and destruction.
The Bull.
The Bull shall destroy him and his beast-friend.
Father, send me the great beast of heaven, the wild Bull.
Death and destruction for this city of pride!

ANU:

>Glorious Ishtar, proud daughter,
>You wish to release the Bull to destroy the city
>You own and its people.
>But have you not quarreled with Gilgamesh,
>Who himself is a great hero?

ISHTAR:

>He has insulted me, a goddess, immortal.
>He has recited my iniquities,
>Spoken to me in bad faith, my lost lovers.
>And he has refused my offer of a sacred marriage
>Before my priestesses, and all the people of Uruk.

ANU:

>But these iniquities – are they not true?
>Is your bad faith not the source of legends?
>Do not your past lovers still roam the earth,
>Or wail in the netherworld and eat the food of the dead?

ISHTAR:

>He has slaughtered my servant, Humbaba of the forest.
>He had defiled the cedar which is sacred to the gods.
>He is proud, concerned only with fame among men,
>Why praise him and make him their god.
>Father, give me the Bull of Heaven.
>Let him devour both Gilgamesh and his friend.
>If you do not, I will smash the gates of the Netherworld.
>I will make the dead rise up and devour the living.
>The dead spirits will overwhelm the earth
>In chaos and confusion.

ANU:

>If I give you the Bull.
>For seven years there will be no harvest.

Have you stored enough grain for the people of Uruk?

Have you grown enough grass for the animals to live?

ISHTAR:

    I have stored enough grain,

    The storehouses are full of wheat

    And dates from the palm trees.

    I have grown enough grass for the animals;

    The animals shall live.

    I can provide for my people.

    But Gilgamesh must die.

ANU:

    So be it.

    Take the wild Bull, whose power is terrible,

    Who destroys in his rage all that comes within his sight.

    Under your name, the results of this act shall be written.

The Bull is formed by the chorus.

1st CITIZEN:

    With the first snort of the Bull, a hole opened I the earth.

    Two hundred young men of Uruk fell in.

    With a flick of its tail, great trees were uprooted.

    Three hundred soldiers were scattered like sand.

    When it bellowed, walls crumbled, and the earth swayed and cracked.

    A great gaping abyss opened at the feet of Enkidu.

    But Enkidu leaped up, seized the Bull by its neck.

ENKIDU:

    We called ourselves heroes when we killed Humbaba;

    But, friend, what can we do with this beast?

GILGAMESH:

    We made our names in the forest;
    Now we'll defend them!

2nd CITIZEN:

    And Enkidu took hold of the horns, with his great strength …

ENKIDU:

    Friend, now I have him! Come, thrust your sword!

1st CITIZEN:

    Gilgamesh grabbed hold of the tail, leaped onto the back,
    And thrust his great sword through the neck of the monster.

GILGAMESH:

    I have done it! He falls!

The Bull groans and falls. The ensemble that created the Bull falls apart. As each person assumes the role of a citizen again, the shape of the slowly Bull disappears. Some citizens cry with joy, while others are stunned with fear.

ISHTAR:

    Curse Gilgamesh, who has dishonored me twice with his arrogance!
    Curse Enkidu, the half-man, who contaminates both city and king!

ENKIDU:

    Proud goddess, you cannot destroy us, together.
    Side by side, we are greater than the terrors of the gods!
    If I could reach you, as I have this bull,
    I would do the same to you! Leave us,
    Queen of harlots! Uruk is ours!
    We shall cover your temple with the entrails and blood!

2nd CITIZEN:

    They cut out the heart, and offered it to Shamash.
    Gilgamesh severed the great horns,

Which were of gleaming lapis lazuli.
The capacity of each was six measures of oil,
Which he offered to his guardian, Lugulbanda.
He took the horns and placed them in his house.
Then the city was filled with great joy and feasting,
And the people praised their heroes:

GILGAMESH:

Who is the greatest of heroes?

CITIZENS:

Gilgamesh!

ENKIDU:

Who has the strength of a thousand?

CITIZENS:

Enkidu!

The celebration moves offstage, revealing the lamenting at the temple of ISHTAR.
The lament carries through the next speech and may include the names of the
gods: EA, ENLIL, SHAMASH, ANU.

OLD GILGAMESH:

The city was joyous, except for the temple of Ishtar.
The goddess and her priestesses began a lamentation over the bull,
And their wailing did not cease.
It must have been Anu who called the gods together.
In their council, they debated, and decided the fate
Of my brother, and me.

END OF SCENE FOUR

SCENE FIVE

The Council of the Gods and the Death of Enkidu

ENLIL:

>Our father had called us
>In sorrow and pain.
>And I hear a lament from the temple of Uruk,
>I have come to discover the source of this discord.
>I am Enlil, protector of the air and the mountains.

EA:

>What is this wailing?
>What does the temple of Ishtar lament?
>I am Ea, god of sweet waters.
>The salt tears of my sister bring me here to learn
>What affront or injustice has raised up this cry.

SHAMASH:

>I am also prepared to consider reasons
>Why our sister laments, what new affront she has suffered.

I am Shamash, the sun god.
Protector of heroes, and giver of light to mankind.

ANU:

You are welcome,
But without pleasure we must gather in council.
The priestesses of Ishtar have set up their lament
Over the loss and destruction of the great Bull of heaven.
A magnificent beast, he held great power in heaven,
And served as a sign of the power of the gods.
Gilgamesh and Enkidu have killed him.
His power was such that no man could withstand him,
But these two, together, showed strength unsurpassed.
They slaughtered the Bull, took the horns to their glory,
And defiled the temple of Ishtar with his blood.

ENLIL:

They have also killed my servant, Humbaba,
And taken sacred wood from my forest as their own.

EA:

If they have killed both the Bull and Humbaba
Their fame among men shall be great.
They shall grow in the legends equal to gods.

ANU:

Because they have slain the Bull, and Humbaba
Because they have insulted the gods, they must die.
The one who stripped the mountain of its cedar
Must die, as the price for his ambition.

ENLIL:

Let Gilgamesh live.
He shall live to regret his transgressions against us.
He shall live yet awhile, and understand death.

Enkidu shall die. His one friend and companion
Shall be to Gilgamesh the image and mirror of death.

SHAMASH:

But why must this be?
Was it not by my order that they killed Humbaba?
Did I not give them the courage to face the wild bull?
And now innocent Enkidu, who only helped his friend,
Should suffer the punishment of the gods who created him?

ENLIL:

It is your fault that they exceeded their bounds in the first place!
Because you, like a comrade, went down daily,
Made yourself their guardian, gave Gilgamesh
A heart restless and proud,
Because of this they repay us with insults and bloodshed.
One shall die – and you are the cause of the death.

SHAMASH:

I will not bear these accusations!
We have created these two, who together
Are beast, man, and god, and whose
Power and courage combine to defy us!
Shall the parents destroy the child who grows up to challenge them?

ANU:

It must be. One shall die.
Royal Ishtar, it is you who have been most offended.
Name the one.

ISHTAR:

Not the king, but his friend.
Gilgamesh will be helpless to protect or defend him
Enkidu will die, in the arms of his brother.

ENKIDU (*awakes from a dream*):

> My brother! Did you call me?
> Then why am I awake?
> I have had a dream; the gods were in council.
> "Because they killed Humbaba," they said,
> "And the bull, one must die."
> Gilgamesh, must it be true?

GILGAMESH:

> Enkidu, this dream means nothing.
> It is an evil, placed in your thoughts by Ishtar.
> I will pray to the gods, to Shamash, for comfort.

ENKIDU (*cries out, stricken by pain*):

> Ah, Gilgamesh, some fire consumes me!
> Yet my legs are like ice, with no power to stand!

OLD GILGAMESH:

> The gods would free me at the cost of my brother?
> But will I never see him again with my eyes?
> How can I protect him from an evil unseen?

GILGAMESH:

> Enkidu, do not give in. Cast away your fear!

ENKIDU:

> I can't fight against it.
> Friend, some god is angry with me.
> I will not die in battle or on the plains, but here in this city
> My life is over.

GILGAMESH:

> Ninsun, goddess, queen, mother.
> Why have I deserved this?
> Why will the gods not help us?

Pray to Shamash for us; pray to Anu.

Intercede on behalf of my brother, Enkidu,

Whom you adopted;

Your son is dying!

NINSUN:

I can do nothing. Anu has decided.

OLD GILGAMESH:

I prayed to the gods to deliver Enkidu from sickness,

But Enkidu did not rise from his bed.

He was thrown down a first day, a second, Enkidu lying on his bed.

A third day and a fourth day, Enkidu is on his bed;

And does not get up.

ENLIL and EA:

Enkidu's limbs lost all strength.

Like lumps of clay, his arms and legs lay

Motionless; his skin wet and cold.

The birds of the air – eagles, vultures, and crows

Would tear at his flesh, and he could not prevent them.

ENKIDU:

I curse that vile trapper, who first saw me on the plains!

Shamash, I beseech you, make his life a misery!

Make his game scarce, make him feeble,

Let his quarry escapes from his nets everyday.

And the woman: with a great curse, I curse her as well!

May she be expelled from the temple forever,

With no place to conduct her vile business!

May she sit in the dust at the crossroads,

And have no roof at night,

May brambles and thorns tear her feet,

And the drunkard strike her mouth in anger.

NINSUN:

> Enkidu, why are you cursing the woman
> The mistress who taught you to eat bread and drink wine?
> Did she not give you magnificent garments,
> Teach you the ways of men, and give you Gilgamesh as a companion?
> And has not Gilgamesh, your brother, given you a royal bed,
> And made the princes of the earth bow before you?
> When you are dead, he will grow his hair long for your sake,
> He will wear the skins of animals, and wander through the desert
> In mourning for you.

OLD GILGAMESH:

> And Enkidu forgave the woman, and took back his curse.
> A fifth day and a sixth he lay on his bed, and did not move.
> A seventh day, an eighth the sickness held him.

NINSUN and ISHTAR (*together*):

> Inside his body a fire raged,
> Though his skin was cold to the touch.
> Vile creatures attacked him: ants, beetles, and scorpions,
> Their bites, like sharp knives cut through his flesh,
> The wounds were invisible, but the pain so strong
> That breath came hard, and the light of his eyes grew dim.

ENKIDU:

> The gate, gate of the forest,
> It has destroyed me now.
> I see you there now, empty of understanding,
> Without power to hear me, yet I speak to you now.
> Twenty leagues away I admired your beauty:
> Your fine wood, your craftsmanship, the hinges of gold.
> Had I known that it would come to this
> I would never have entered.
> Someone else should have penetrated that gate way,
> And taken the curse from me.

OLD GILGAMESH:

> A ninth and a tenth day, Enkidu lay sick, his body weak and bleeding.
> An eleventh day, a twelfth day Enkidu suffered in sickness,
> And I was helpless to comfort him.

ANU:

> The things of the earth – worms, lizards, and snakes,
> Which feed on the dead now infested his body.
> His flesh, which once gleamed alongside the gazelles,
> Was now rancid, useless, and full of disease.
> The bellows of Enkidu's lungs could now barely move his breath.
> Blood filled his mouth, though his tongue was dry.
> His eyes, once star-like, would not open,
> But his brain was split by a chaos of light.

ENKIDU:

> Friend, I saw a dream in the night.
> The heavens groaned, the earth resounded, between them
> I stood alone.
> There was a man, his face was dark.
> The paws of a lion were his paws; the talons of the eagle were his
> talons.
> He grabbed my hair and overpowered me,
> And let me down to the house of darkness,
> Where they live in dust, and dust is their food.
> They see no light, living in blackness.
> I saw Ereshkigal, the queen of that place.
> The scribe of the underworld kneels beside her;
> She holds a tablet and reads to the queen.
> And the queen, lifting her head, looked directly at me; she said:
> "Who has brought this one here?"

OLD and YOUNG GILGAMESH (*together*):

> What is this sleep that has taken hold of you?
> You are dark, you can't hear me!

OLD GILGAMESH:

    I touched his heart. It did not beat.

    Enkidu did not lift his head.

    Like a lioness whose whelps are lost, I paced back and forth,

    Tearing my hair.

    Like an eagle, I circled over him.

    He did not rise, he did not move.

    I covered my friend's face, like a bride's.

MUSIC: "The Citizens Mourn Enkidu's Death"

OLD and YOUNG GILGAMESH (*together*):

    And I was alone.

ANU and the GODS (*staggered*):

    And Gilgamesh was alone.

END SCENE FIVE

SCENE SIX

The Journey to Utnapishtim

Tableau of previous scene dissolves, except for ISHTAR and GILGAMESH, and two PRIESTESSES.

ISHTAR:

> The city was filled with great mourning
> And loudest of all was King Gilgamesh.
> He wailed over his friend
> And the elders and people of Uruk
> Joined in his suffering.

GILGAMESH:

> Enkidu was the axe at my side,
> The bow at my arm, the shield in front of me.
> He was my festive garment, my splendid attire.
> Now I will throw off my clothes,
> Their beauty insults me.

I will wear the skins of animals
And wander in the desert for my friend.

1st CITIZEN:

The desert shall weep for him.

CHORUS:

Their dry sands cry out.

2nd CITIZEN:

The meadows shall weep for him.

CHORUS:

Their green grasses mourning.

3rd CITIZENS:

The beasts of the plain, tigers and antelopes
All mourn the loss of their friend.

CHORUS:

The deer, the hyena, the bull and the panther
All weep for the loss of their brother.

4th CITIZEN:

The river Euphrates, where you took fresh water.

CHORUS:

Swells with sighs and tears at your death.

5th CITIZEN:

In the cedar forest every tree and each pathway.

CHORUS:

All mourn. The weeping does not end day or night.

ISHTAR:

Gilgamesh lay in his bed – but he could not sleep.
He thought of his friend, and of death

And a cold fear entered him
And would not subside.

GILGAMESH:
Enkidu has gone to the world of the spirits.
Can no one enter there and challenge the god of the dead?
And what of me? Will I not die, too?
How can I rest? How can I be at peace?
What my brother is now, so shall I be.
Strength and kingship the gods gave me, but not immortality.
The secret they keep for themselves.

1st PRIESTESS OF ISHTAR:
Except one.

2nd PRIESTESS OF ISHTAR:
Except one.

1st PRIESTESS OF ISHTAR:
Utnapishtim.

2nd PRIESTESS OF ISHTAR:
Utnapishtim.

1st PRIESTESS OF ISHTAR:
Utnapishtim, the faraway, who lived before the flood.

2nd PRIESTESS OF ISHTAR:
The gods saved him and granted him the secret of life.

1st PRIESTESS OF ISHTAR:
He lives forever, at the end of the earth.
At the source of the rivers, and the gate of the underworld.

2nd PRIESTESS OF ISHTAR:
Beyond the mountains of Mashu, in the garden of the sun.

1st PRIESTESS OF ISHTAR:
>   Only he knows the secret.

2nd PRIESTESS OF ISHTAR:
>   But no man can go there.

1st PRIESTESS OF ISHTAR:
>   It is far.

2nd PRIESTESS OF ISHTAR:
>   It is far.

1st PRIESTESS OF ISHTAR:
>   And the danger is great.

2nd PRIESTESS OF ISHTAR:
>   Do not go, Gilgamesh

1st PRIESTESS OF ISHTAR:
>   Do not go.

2nd PRIESTESS OF ISHTAR:
>   It is far.

1st PRIESTESS OF ISHTAR:
>   It is dangerous.

1st PRIESTESS OF ISHTAR:
>   You will not return.

GILGAMESH:
>   How can I rest? How can I be at peace?
>   The friend I loved has turned to clay.
>   What my brother is now, so shall I be.
>   I shall go to Utnapishtim,
>   Whom the gods have preserved from death,

He will tell me the secret of life,
Show me the entrance to the house of the dead,
And I shall return with Enkidu.

OLD GILGAMESH:

The mountains of Mashu stand at the end of the world.

The ensemble forms scorpion gate.

There the sun rises from his dwelling beyond,
In the garden of the gods.
No one had ever passed through the mountains
For the passage is terrifying
And the gate is guarded by great scorpions.
I traveled there, and I heard them as I drew near the gate:

SCORPION MAN:

This one who comes is not like other men.

SCORPION WOMAN:

This one who comes, his body is flesh of the gods.

SCORPION MAN:

He is two thirds god.

SCORPION WOMAN:

He is one third man.

SCORPION MAN:

This one is bold.

SCORPION WOMAN:

But carries fear in his heart.

OLD GILGAMESH:

Their terror was awesome, their eyes like hot glowing stones.

Their shadows were cast up the mountains
Whose peaks reached the heavens
And whose base was in the underworld.
My heart filled with fear,
But still I approached them.

SCORPION MAN:

Why have you come here to this end of all journeys?
What is it you wish?
Who are you, who stand before these gates of darkness?

GILGAMESH:

I come for Enkidu, my friend, who is dead.
We endured many hardships together
And made ourselves a name among men.
I wish to bring him back from the house of the dead.
I am in search of Utnapishtim,
For men say he has entered the assembly of gods
And knows the secret of life.

SCORPION WOMAN:

No one has endured what you wish to do.
No one has crossed through these mountains of Shamash.
The length of the path is twelve leagues.
From the rising of the sun to the setting of the sun
There is no light.
Your heart will be oppressed by utter darkness.

GILGAMESH:

If I must go in sorrow and pain
Still I will enter into the mountain.
How can I rest? How can I be at peace
When my brother is dead?

SCORPION MAN:

>Go, Gilgamesh, the gate is open to you.
>
>May your feet bring you back to your homeland.

SCORPION WOMAN:

>He traveled one league and the darkness was thick.
>
>He saw nothing ahead and nothing behind him.
>
>After two leagues the darkness was thick
>
>And there was no light.
>
>He saw nothing ahead and nothing behind him.

BOTH SCORPIONS:

>After three leagues the darkness was thick
>
>And there was no light.
>
>He saw nothing ahead and nothing behind him.
>
>After four leagues the darkness was thick
>
>And there was no light.
>
>Gilgamesh saw nothing ahead and nothing behind him.

BOTH SCORPIONS AND OTHER VOICES:

>At the end of five leagues, the darkness was thick
>
>And there was no light.
>
>He saw nothing ahead and nothing behind him.
>
>At the end of six leagues, the darkness was thick
>
>And there was no light.
>
>He saw nothing ahead and nothing behind him.

ADD ONE MORE VOICE:

>At the end of seven leagues, the darkness was thick
>
>And there was no light.
>
>He saw nothing ahead and nothing behind him
>
>At the end of eight leagues Gilgamesh gave a great cry,
>
>For the darkness has entered his soul.

MORE VOICES:

>At the end of nine leagues he felt the north wind on his face,
>But the darkness was thick and there was no light.
>At the end of ten leagues the end was near.

OTHER VOICES:

>At the end of eleven leagues the dawn light appeared.
>At the end of twelve leagues the sunlight streamed out,
>And Gilgamesh entered the garden of the gods.

The ensemble becomes garden of the gods. MUSIC: "Music of the Garden of the Gods."

OLD GILGAMESH:

>The garden was magnificent, like nothing ever seen.
>It was filled with lush greenery,
>But the bushed bore not fruit, but fine gems.

TREE:

>There was a tree with fruit of carnelian,
>Its branches aglow with the translucent gems.

VINE:

>A vine whose great leaves were of lapis lazuli,
>Deep blue in the sunlight, and glistening with gold.

THISTLES and BRIARS:

>Thistles and briars bore sweet pearls and rare stones,
>Their riches protected by ebony thorns.

FLOWERS:

>There were flowers with petals of ivory and jade,
>Violets of amethyst, with alabaster leaves.

OLD GILGAMESH:

> I walked to the edge of the sea, whose waves glistened
> With the brightness of silver
> And I heard Shamash speak to me:

SHAMASH:

> Gilgamesh, why do you wander by the edge of the sea
> Dressed in the skins of animals, your face worn and weary?
> No mortal has ever walked this path.
> Your quest is fruitless.
> You will never find the life you seek.
> Go back to your city, and be content.

GILGAMESH:

> I have come this far; am I to sleep now
> And let the earth cover my head, like Enkidu?
> Let my eyes see the sun, although they are blind.

OLD GILGAMESH:

> And so on I traveled, along the strand of the sea
> Where Shamash sleeps, until I came the house of Siduri,
> The maker of wine.

GILGAMESH approaches Siduri, but she tries to lock her gate against him.

GILGAMESH:

> Young woman, mistress of wine,
> Why do you bar your door against me?
> Let me in, for I am Gilgamesh, who killed the bull of heaven,
> Who conquered the cedar forest.

SIDURI:

> If you are that Gilgamesh, why are your cheeks sunken
> And your eyes unclear?

Why is your face like the face of one who has made a long journey?
What do you seek here?

GILGAMESH:

Why should my cheeks not be sunken and my eyes unclear?
My face is the face of one who has made a long journey,
For I have traveled across the plains and the deserts, followed the wind.
I am seeking Utnapishtim the faraway, whom the gods
Have preserved from death.
My friend, Enkidu, endured many dangers beside me;
He is dead.
For twelve days he lay on his bed; now he dwells in the underworld.
I will go down there to rescue him.
Utnapishtim will show me the way,
And tell me the secret of life.

SIDURI:

But Gilgamesh, why do you journey in the wilderness?
You will never find the life you seek.
When the gods created man, they gave him death,
And everlasting life they kept for themselves.
Therefore, Gilgamesh, fill yourself with good food;
Each day make a feast of rejoicing.
Dance and play both day and night,
Let your garments be fresh, and your hair
Washed with clean water.
Enjoy the child who takes you by the hand,
And sleep soundly in the arms of your wife.

GILGAMESH:

How can I rest? How can I be at peace?
What my brother is now, so shall I be.
Siduri, show me the way to Utnapishtim.
Where is the passage? In what direction?
I will not rest until I speak with him.

SIDURI:

>He lives beyond the waters of death,
>But no man has ever crossed that sea.
>The water is dark and its touch poison.
>But, Gilgamesh, down in the forest
>You will find Urshanabi.
>He is the ferryman for Utnapishtim and his wife.
>With him, perhaps you could cross the black waters.

OLD GILGAMESH:

>I took my axe in my hand, and my dagger from my belt,
>I prowled through the forest, to the boatman Urshanabi.
>From behind him, I could see that he was fashioning some weapons.
>So I crept forward silently, and descended quickly upon him,
>Smashing his head and destroying his weapons.

URSHANABI:

>Ahhh! Who is this who attacks me?
>What do you want from a simple boatman?

GILGAMESH:

>I am Gilgamesh, who killed the bull of heaven,
>Who conquered the cedar forest.
>I have come to speak with Utnapishtim,
>And you will take me across the waters of death.

URSHANABI:

>If you are that Gilgamesh, why are your cheeks sunken
>And your eyes unclear?
>Why is your face like the face of one who has made a long journey?
>You carry a sorrow within you, and an evil
>Follows you on your journey,
>And yet you would speak with Utnapishtim,
>Who lives in assembly with the gods.

GILGAMESH:

> It is not for my sake that I have wandered
> Through the deserts and mountains,
> But for the sake of my friend, who is dead.
> How can I rest? How can I be at peace?
> The friend I loved, has gone to the underworld.
> I will never see him again.
> I cannot rescue him without the wisdom of Utnapishtim.
> If there is a way across the waters of death, tell me now!

URSHANABI:

> Gilgamesh, you are impulsive and rash.
> Like a fool you have destroyed the means of your own crossing.
> Those were not weapons I was fashioning,
> But rudder and tackle to take the boat across the sea.
> If we go now, we go without guidance.

GILGAMESH:

> My journey cannot wait. Each day I delay Enkidu
> Becomes more like the dead who surround him.
> We shall cross the waters together.
> You will show me the way.

URSHANABI:

> Go, Gilgamesh, cut poles in the forest.
> One hundred and twenty, cut straight and strong,
> And bring them to me.

GILGAMESH:

> Here they are: one hundred and twenty;
> But how will these help us?

URSHANABI:

> We'll put the raft in the water, Gilgamesh,

But do not let it touch you.
With the poles we will push ourselves safely across.

The ensemble forms the water, they board the raft and use the poles to cross the waters.

URSHANABI:
Take the first pole, Gilgamesh, and thrust it in deeply.
Do not let your hands touch the waters of death.
Take a second pole, Gilgamesh, and thrust it in deeply.
Do not let your hands touch the waters of death.
Take a third and a fourth pole, and thrust them in deeply.
Do not let your hands touch the waters of death.
Take a fifth and a sixth pole, and thrust them in deeply.
Do not let your hands touch the waters of death.
A seventh and eighth , a ninth and a tenth pole,
Now thrust them in deeply.
Do not let your hands touch the waters of death.
An eleventh and twelfth pole, now thrust them in deeply.
Do not let your hands touch the waters of death.

OLD GILGAMESH:
So I punted the raft across the waters of death,
Until the poles had all been used.
We could see the shore of Utnapishtim in the distance,
So I took off my clothes and held them out for the wind,
Like a sail, they carried us to shore.

UTNAPISHTIM:
Who has sent this one here?
Why does the ferryman not control the boat?
This one who comes is not one of mine.

MRS. UTNAPISHTIM:
This one who comes is flesh of the gods.

UTNAPISHTIM:

    What is your name, you who come here wearing the skins of animals?

    Why are your cheeks sunken and your eyes unclear?

    Why is your face like the face of one who has made a long journey?

    Tell me the reason for your coming.

GILGAMESH:

    I am Gilgamesh, who killed the bull of heaven,

    Who conquered the cedar forest.

    I have come to speak with Utnapishtim,

    Because my friend, Enkidu, whom I loved, has died,

    And I shall be like him.

    I have crossed mountains and deserts,

    And treacherous oceans.

    I have worn myself out wandering,

    No sleep has calmed my face.

    My clothes are ragged, and my cheeks are hollow.

    Utnapishtim, the gods have granted you life everlasting.

    Only you have overcome death, only you know the secret.

    Tell me, how can I overcome death, and rescue my friend?

    Tell me, how shall I find the life I am seeking?

UTNAPISHTIM:

    There is no permanence.

    Does the house we build stand forever?

    Does a contract bind for all time?

    Does hostility last forever between enemies?

    Does trust never die among friends?

    From the very beginning, there was no permanence.

    Nothing remains but time.

    The sleeping and the dead, how like brothers they are!

    The primitive man and the hero both share the same fate.

    The gods of destiny set the ends of things;

    They settle death and life.

The time of life is clear to all;
As for death, its time is hidden.

GILGAMESH:

But death is not hidden!
Enkidu, my brother, lay sick on his bed
For twelve days.
He neither ate nor walked.
His body grew weak, until his breath stopped.
Now I must go down to the underworld
To bring back my friend, and you must show me
The way, and tell me the secret of the return.

UTNAPISHTIM:

It is not possible.
There is no returning for the souls of the dead.
No man who crosses that gate can come back to the land of the living.
And Enkidu was a man, as you, Gilgamesh, are a man.

GILGAMESH:

But I look at you, Utnapishtim,
And your features are no different than mine.
I am like you.
Yet you live here, timeless, at the source of the rivers
And never grow old.
You will not face death, as I have seen Enkidu face it.
Oh, how can I rest? How can I be at peace?
What my brother is now, so shall I be.
Men live, and die, and are forgotten,
Their bodies returning to the clay of the riverbank,
The memory of their deeds washed away in the current.
You, Utnapishtim, were granted eternal life by the gods.
I am at the end of my journey.
Tell me, what must I do to be saved from death?

UTNAPISHTIM:

> You wish to conquer death. First test yourself.
> Conquer sleep first of all.
> Stay here with me, and watch without sleep for six days
> And seven nights.
> Conquer sleep first, then perhaps I will tell you the secret of life.

GILGAMESH *falls asleep.*

UTNAPISHTIM (*to his wife*):

> Look at this hero who asks for life!
> Sleep pours down on him like honey.

MRS. UTNAPISHTIM:

> Touch him, so he'll wake up.
> He'll return on his way, and go in peace,
> Back to his people and his homeland.

UTNAPISHTIM:

> A man who is trouble will give trouble.
> He will deny that he ever slept.
> Bake loaves of bread, one each day he sleeps,
> And set them beside his head,
> So that when he wakes, he will see how time has fooled him.

END SCENE SIX

SCENE SEVEN

The Secret of Immortality

GILGAMESH asleep. MUSIC: "Music of Sleep/Sickness." UTNAPISHTIM touches him, and he wakes suddenly.

GILGAMESH:

    I wasn't sleeping! I had only closed my eyes when you touched me!

UTNAPISHTIM:

    Come, Gilgamesh! Observe these loaves,
    One for every day you have slept.
    The first is still warm, but the second is like leather,
    The third has mildewed, the fourth grows mold,
    The fifth is all grey, the sixth is stiff,
    And the seventh crumbles to dust.
    This is how sleep overcame you.
    And you wanted to conquer death!

GILGAMESH:

    What am I to do? Where can I go?

Some evil has come and robbed me.

Death lives in my home.

Everywhere I turn, there death waits.

Have I traveled this journey for nothing?

UTNAPISHTIM:

Urshanabi, you will no longer cross the waters.

After this, the harbor will reject you.

The shore will be denied you.

No one shall see this place again.

As for this man, his trials have obscured his beauty.

Take him to the washing place;

Throw off his animal skins,

Let him wash his hair in clean water;

Let the goodness of his body shine out.

Give him new garments, the garments of an elder,

That he may return to his city with dignity.

MRS. UTNAPISHTIM:

Gilgamesh has suffered and toiled to come here.

He killed lions in the mountain passes,

Journeyed through ten leagues of darkness,

Crossed the waters of death, all to meet with you.

What have you given him in return?

UTNAPISHTIM:

He will return safely. That is enough.

MRS. UTNAPISHTIM:

Is it? This king, part god and part man,

Who has killed Humbaba and the Bull of Heaven,

Who has watched his brother face death,

Shall he return to his city with nothing?

UTNAPISHTIM:

Gilgamesh, you have suffered and toiled to come here,
You have killed lions, gone through darkness,
And crossed the waters of death.
No man will follow after you.
I will reveal to you a secret of the gods,
There is a plant.
Its roots grow deep.
And its thorns will cut your hands like knives.
It grows at the bottom of the deep river bed,
Where Ea dwells, at the source of clear water.
If you can get that plant, you will have life everlasting.

GILGAMESH:

Come, Urshanabi!
I will tie great stones to my ankles
So that I can walk beneath the water of the river bed.
I will find the plant, and we will return to Uruk.

He does so. Ensemble becomes water again, this time the river. GILGAMESH
finds the plant, cuts away the stones, and surfaces.

URSHANABI:

Do you have it? Gilgamesh!
Could you see it?

GILGAMESH:

I have it! The plant of life! I have it!
Urshanabi, this is the plant which gives men youth within.
I will carry it to Uruk,
And I will give it to the elders, to divide among themselves.
Then I will eat it, too, and I will return to
The life I had in my youth,
Without pain, without anguish,

When every day was a festival,
Without fear of death.
Every citizen of Uruk will partake of this plant.
We shall neither see nor suffer death again.

GILGAMESH and URSHANABI set off. Shift focus to group listening to OLD GILGAMESH.

OLD GILGAMESH:

We traveled across the waters, like two young heroes.
We came to the shore, walked twenty leagues and then
Had something to eat.
Another thirty and we stopped for the night.

GILGAMESH and URSHANABI reappear, mime the following in dim light.

GILGAMESH:

I saw a pool of clear water,
Quiet and glistening under willows.
I stripped off my clothes and went down to bathe.
Leaving the flowered plant on the bank of moss.
In the bottom of the black pool, something stirred.
A great serpent lived there, coiled upon itself.
It rose up, smelling the sweet scent of the flower.
It came up through the water, brushing past me,
And like a demon from the underworld, it stole the plant away,
Carrying it to the bottom of the pool.
I tried to pursue it, but the black water closed around me.
I could not find the bottom; the pool's depth was unending.
I had no more breath, and returned to the air.
There on the bank, where the flower had been,
I saw that the serpent has thrown off his skin.

OLD GILGAMESH:

>That day, I sat down, weeping.
>
>That day, the tears flowed over my face.
>
>My heart was black and empty.

GILGAMESH:

>I cried out to Shamash;
>
>For whom have my arms been tested?
>
>For what has the blood of my heart dried up?
>
>I have journeyed and labored, am worn out and weary
>
>For nothing.
>
>I have won no good for myself.
>
>I have nothing for my city.
>
>The plant was the sign I had longed for,
>
>The life for which I was searching.
>
>I had a sign, and it was taken away from me.

GILGAMESH and OLD GILGAMESH:

>I had a sign, and it was taken away from me.

OLD GILGAMESH:

>I returned to Uruk. To my home.
>
>I had nothing.
>
>Since the death of Enkidu,
>
>On my long journey, I have been to the end of the earth.
>
>I have seen mysteries, learned secrets.
>
>I have seen the abyss, the secret and terror of life.
>
>And I have brought back nothing – but my story.
>
>Gilgamesh is nothing, but this story.
>
>And this story is yours.
>
>I have given it to you.

MUSIC: "Music of the Waters of Death" – a solitary flute. A slow, melancholy beginning as the citizens (wedding guests from scene one) are gathered around OLD GILGAMESH. MUSIC: "Wedding Song No. 2." The music gradually gets faster and brighter, percussion is added, and the dancing celebration of the wedding resumes, including the old man. No one needs to speak. The stage is filled with dancing.

All exeunt through vomitorium, except for ISHTAR.

END SCENE SEVEN

GILGAMESH CON/QUEST

The epic dramatized in seven scenes

Original Music

by Wendy Balder

A Hero Has Come

Original Music: Wendy Balder

Dance, Dance, Dance!

Original Music: Wendy Balder

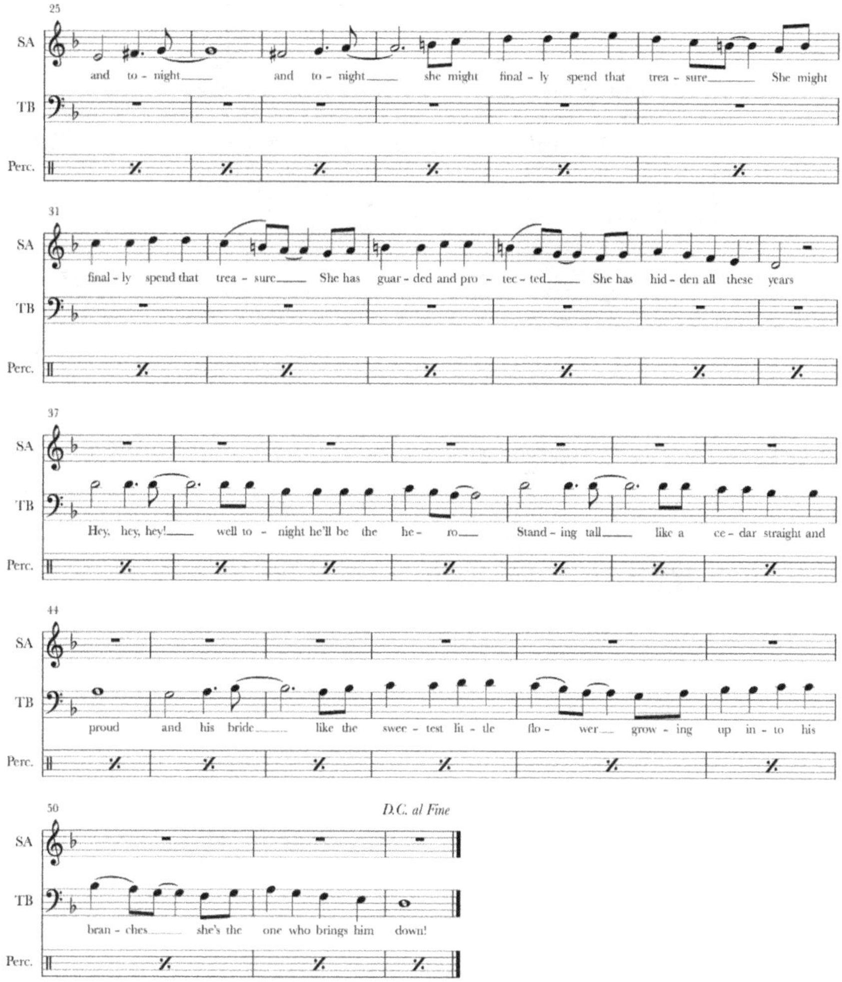

The Woman Speaks To Enkidu

Original Music: Wendy Balder

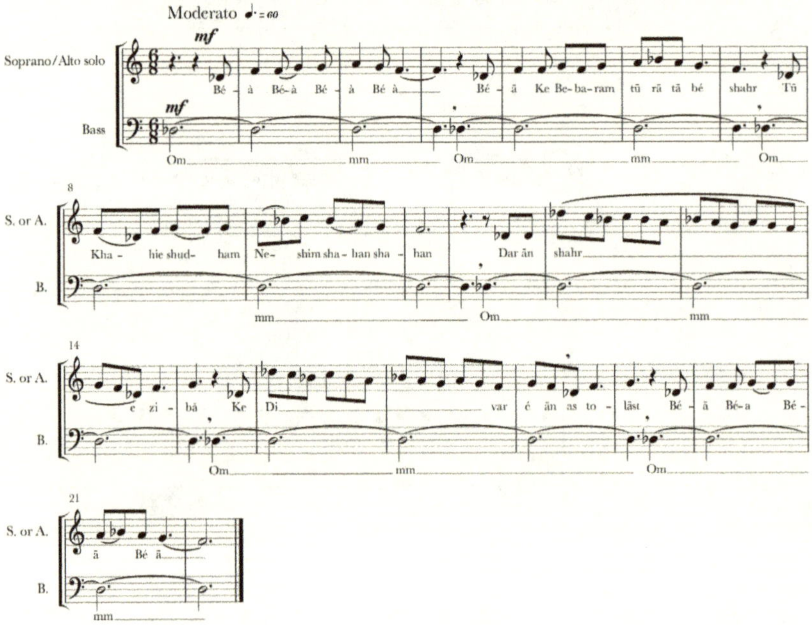

A Hero Has Come

Original Music: Wendy Balder

Tenor Solo
A He – ro has come to stand next to Gil – ga – mesh.
Pries – tess of Ish – tar has brought him to U – ruk.

Chorus of Men
Wel – come En – ki – du Friend to the King

Solo
A
Chorus of Men
We sing for the ci – ty we sing for the friend! We
We sing for the ci – ty we sing for the friend! We

145

Rejoicing Over Gilgamesh and Enkidu's Triumph Over Humbaba.

long   live the   names of   en- ki   du

long   live the   names of   En- ki   du -

long   live the   names of   En- k   du

repeat once-more   *repeat several times*

and hum—   ba   ba long   en-ki-du! Gil-ga-mesh!

and hum—   ba—   ba, long   en-ki-du! Gil-ga-mesh!

and hum—   ba—   ba, long   enki du! Gil-ga-mesh!

ba· long   en-ki-du!

Song of Ishtar's Seduction + Gilgamesh's Rejection

Original Music: Wendy Balder

33
A.
de- mons of wind like de- mons of wind like the de- mons of
T.
Perc.
39
Tutti
1.
2.
wind Prin- ces and ru- lers and kings shall bow be-fore you you The glo-
47
ry of U- ruk is yours of U- ruk is yours of U- ruk is yours and
54
mine Lie with me un- der cool palms with
(Gilgamesh's part optional)
No! Keep a - way from me Your love is a trea - che - ry
59
Repeat again
sweet fra - grance with me with me!
Which one of your lo- vers still lives? No! Keep a - way!

Ishtar's Revenge

Original Music: Wendy Balder

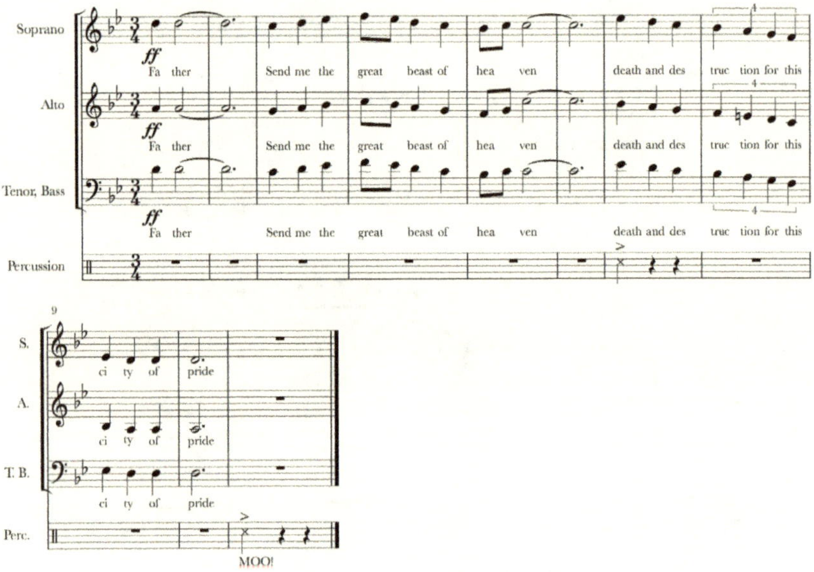

The Citizens Mourn Enkidu's Death

Original Music: Wendy Balder

[score continues on following pages]

151

The Citizens Mourn Enkidu's Death - cont.

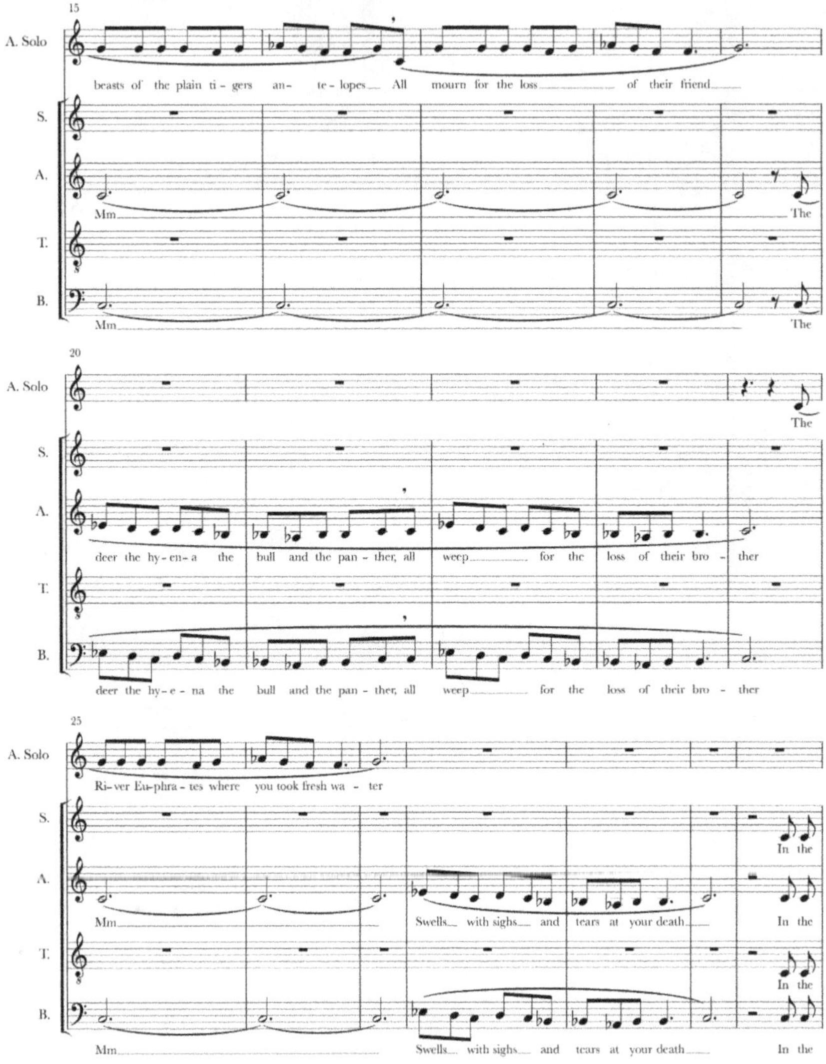

32
A. Solo
S.
A.
T.
B.
Text
Ce- dar fo - rest e - v'ry tree and each path - way all mourn The wee - ping does not
38
1.
2.
end day or night The

Music of the Garden of the Gods

Original Music: Wendy Balder

Music of Sleep/Sickness

Original Music: Wendy Balder

Largo ♩ = 90
[repeat ad libitum]

Recommendation:

To remedy the difficulty of
tuning the four parts when
singing unaccompanied, the
voices should enter as follows:

1) Basses

2) Altos (monotone)

3) Sopranos

4) Tenors (doubling sopranos at
8ba)

The same thing would apply for
the Music of the Waters of Death.

Music of the Waters of Death

Original Music: Wendy Balder

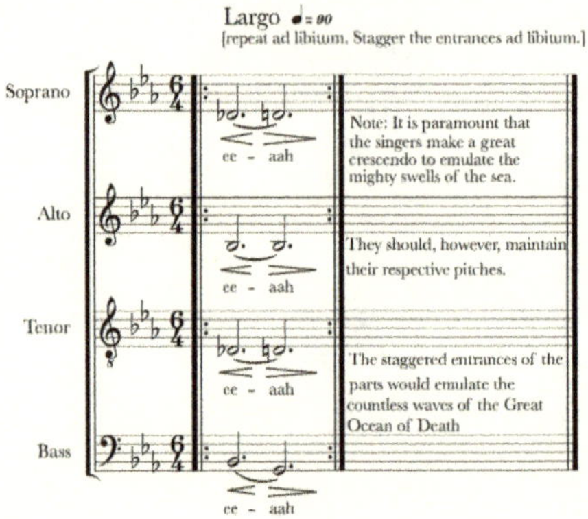

Wedding Song No. 2

Original Music: Wendy Balder

About the Authors

Mahmood Karimi Hakak

A poet, author, translator, and playwright whose scholarly and artistic works are focused on intercultural dialogue and peacebuilding, Karimi Hakak has created over 70 stage and screen production in the U.S., Europe and his native Iran. He has published five plays, two books of poetry, four translations, and numerous articles and interviews. His play *Is the One I Love Everywhere?* (FCI Press 2020) envisions a dialogue between Jalal-al Din Rumi and Forough Farrokhzad. His translation of Hafez, *Your Lover's Beloved*, (CCC Poetry Press 2009) was nominated for the Best Translation of Poetry by the American Literary Translators Association. His most recent book *Shakespeare in Tehran* (Routledge 2023) reviews an encounter with Iranian youth which changed his ten-day visit in 1992 to a seven years residency. Professor Karimi Hakak has taught at Rutgers, Towson, and Southern Methodist universities in the U.S., and University of Tehran, Soore University, and Teachers Training College in Iran. He presently serves as Professor of Creative Arts at Siena College in upstate New York.

Ralph Blasting

Ralph Blasting was the Dean of Visual and Performing Arts at the State University of New York at Fredonia from 2013 to 2019. Prior to that he held positions at Siena College and at Towson University as an administrator and professor of theatre history. He has published on the European theatre of the Middle Ages and has directed a number of college productions. His is currently retired and living in Canada.

Michael B. Dick

A distinguished Professor of Hebrew Bible in the Religious Studies Department at Siena College, Professor Dick has dedicated his academic career to exploring the Hebrew Bible within the broader context of the ancient Near East, providing valuable insights into the cultural and historical connections between these ancient texts and their surrounding civilizations. As an editor, he has contributed significantly to the field with works such as "Born in Heaven, Made on Earth" (Eisenbrauns, 1999), which delves into the complex interplay between divine and human realms in ancient Mesopotamian thought. His research often highlights the intricate relationships between the Hebrew Bible and Mesopotamian literature, shedding light on how these texts influenced each other. Professor Dick's work is highly regarded for its depth and scholarly rigor, making him a prominent figure in the study of ancient Near Eastern history and religion.

Cheryl De Ciantis

Artist, mythologist, writer, educator, and values-based dialogue mentor, De Ciantis has pioneered integrative, arts-based methods in organizational and individual learning and creativity. Her primary training is in art history and historiography, and she holds a PhD in Mythological Studies with Emphasis in Depth Psychology from Pacifica Graduate Institute. Her special area of interest has been the intersection between art, technology and culture in myth, which she explored in her book *The Return of Hephaistos: Reconstructing the Fragmented Mythos of the Makers* (Kairios Press, 2019). She resides in Tucson, Arizona.

Wendy Balder

Composer and educator, Balder graduated from Towson University with a degree in music in 1992. She presently teaches music in Baltimore, Maryland.

Kairios Press

Kairios, similarly to kairos, is an ancient Greek word meaning, roughly, "being in the right place at the right time." The ancient Greeks envisioned both the spiritual and practical essence of kairios by using an image familiar to students of Zen: the archer whose attention is both focused and diffused as she becomes one with the arrow, its flight, and the vital heart of the target. Another Greek image for kairios is that of the weaver who passes his shuttle between the ever-moving threads of the warp with the perfect timing born of holistically integrated rhythm to create something of beauty, organic strength and essential, practical utility. Kairios was co-founded in 2001 by Cheryl De Ciantis, PhD and Kenton Hyatt, PhD.

Visit kairios.com to learn more.

www.ingramcontent.com/pod-product-compliance
Lightning Source LLC
LaVergne TN
LVHW011235080426
835509LV00005B/513